ENFIELD PAST

This book is dedicated
to the memory of my fellow local historian and friend,
Alan Dumayne (1929-1998)

The Illustrations
All the illustrations in this book are reproduced
by kind permission of the London Borough of Enfield

First published 1999
by Historical Publications Ltd
32 Ellington Street, London N7 8PL
(Tel: 020-7607 1628)

© **Graham Dalling, 1999**

ISBN 0 948667 57 5
British Library Cataloguing-in-Publication Data
A catalogue record for this book is available from the British Library

Typeset in Palatino by Historical Publications
Reproduction by G & J Graphics, London EC2
Printed by Edelvives, Zaragoza, Spain

ENFIELD PAST

Graham Dalling

HISTORICAL PUBLICATIONS

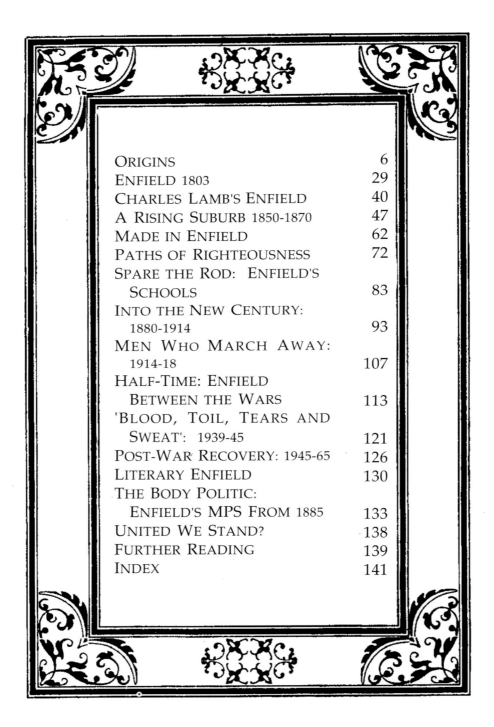

Foreword

Enfield has received almost an excess of attention from local historians in recent years with no less than five full-length hardback books written by my friend and former colleague, David Pam. This book is a single-volume concise history, which concentrates heavily on those forces and events that have helped to shape modern Enfield. Hopefully, it will serve as an introduction to Enfield history for those who have neither the time nor the inclination to read more scholarly works.

Many people have assisted during the preparation of this book. I would particularly like to record my debt to David Pam and also to Geoffrey Gillam. I discussed some of the earlier chapters with Alan Dumayne, to whose memory this book is dedicated – sadly he did not live to see the finished product. I would particularly like to thank Lord Harris of High Cross for taking the trouble to read my account of the Enfield comprehensive education dispute and making some very helpful suggestions. My late grandfather, Harry Ford (1890-1979) could not have realised what he was unleashing when he shared his memories of his Enfield childhood – unfortunately, only a few of his stories are suitable for polite readers.

I would particularly like to record my gratitude to my colleagues Kate Godfrey and Maureen Austin whose help with the preparation of the typescript has been invaluable. (Sadly, owing to Enfield Council's financial problems, one of them will have been made redundant before this book is published.)

Any errors that remain in this book are mine and mine alone. I would stress that the opinions expressed are mine and not those of my employer.

Graham Dalling

1. *The Enfield Manor House (the Palace) in 1778. The site had been occupied since early medieval times.*

Origins

THE LIE OF THE LAND

Enfield lies in the extreme north-east corner of the old county of Middlesex, directly north of Edmonton. Its eastern boundary is formed by the River Lee, on the opposite bank of which lie the Essex parishes of Chingford and Waltham Abbey. To the north, across the Hertfordshire border, Enfield directly abuts the parishes of Cheshunt and Northaw. Along its western boundary, Enfield adjoins East Barnet (Hertfordshire) and the Middlesex parishes of Monken Hadley and South Mimms.

The highest ground lies on the western side from where it slopes down to the floor of the Lee Valley. The River Lee today is a fairly sluggish affair, much reduced by over-abstraction to quench the thirst of London, and straitjacketed by flood prevention measures. However, the sheer dimensions of the valley suggest that in the past the river had been a much mightier affair. It had its origins at the end of the last ice age when the water from melting glaciers was escaping to the sea, in the process depositing large amounts of silt and gravel. (The Lee Valley gravel deposits have been extensively worked to feed the demands of the construction industry. The evidence of large-scale abstraction of gravel and brickearth is written large on Enfield's landscape.)

On the eastern side of the parish, between the Hertford Road and the Lee, the land was low-lying and, close to the river, prone to flooding; it was mostly used as grazing land. The main area of arable land lay between the Hertford Road and the Enfield Town/Bulls Cross axis where the soil, well-drained and friable brickearth, if well manured, was capable of producing good crops of grain. Significantly, this area was one of the last parts of Enfield to be built upon. The high ground of Enfield Chase remained heavily wooded into fairly recent times and the soil, a heavy clay, even with modern farming equipment, has never been particularly good agricultural land.

The other local watercourses all drain directly or indirectly into the Lee. Pymmes Brook rises in the Hadley Wood area and runs through East Barnet, Southgate and Upper Edmonton before joining the Lee at Tottenham. Salmons Brook rises on Enfield Chase, passing under Hadley Road and Slades Hill, before crossing into Edmonton near Bush Hill and joining Pymmes Brook near Angel Road Station. Turkey Brook and its various tributaries rise across the border in Hertfordshire. It passes beneath Whitewebbs Lane, Flash Lane and

2. *A section of the Old River Lee on the Enfield/Edmonton border in 1903, showing the river in its natural state. The site is now under the Girling Reservoir.*

Maidens Bridge before running alongside Turkey Street and beneath the Hertford Road at the Woolpack Bridge to join the Lee near the Royal Small Arms Factory. (The present course between the Woolpack Bridge and the Lee is an artificial cut probably made in the early nineteenth century. The old course ran south alongside the Hertford Road, before swinging eastwards across the marshes close to Bell Lane.) The Saddlers Mill Stream rises close to the northern end of Chase Side, passing under Parsonage Lane and the New River and across what is now the Enfield Grammar School playing field. Crossing Holly Walk, it runs beneath Church Street close to the main Post Office and then across what is now the Town Park. It then goes under London Road, Village Road and Wellington Road and winds a circuitous course through the Bury Street/Bounces Road area of Edmonton before linking up with Salmons Brook. This watercourse has now almost entirely disappeared from view, having been culverted for most of its length, though a short stretch still runs open through Bush Hill Park which can be seen from Wellington Road and Village Road. At one time this stream was the principal source of drinking water and yet the main drainage for the Enfield Town area.

THE ROMAN ERA

Archaeological finds provide evidence of an early human presence in the area. Flint implements were discovered during the construction of the George V Reservoir and a flint scraper was recovered from a garden in Connaught Avenue. In 1952 the remains of a dugout canoe were found in the course of gravel digging at Ramney Marsh and in 1960 the same location yielded up a bronze sword and spearhead.

In AD43 the Roman armies under the Emperor Claudius began the conquest of Britain. Within a very short time much of southern England was firmly under their control and major settlements were established at London (Londinium), Colchester (Camulodunum) and St Albans (Verulamium). In AD60, while the principal Roman armies were engaged in the suppression of British resistance in North Wales and Anglesey, disaster struck. Boudicca, queen of the Iceni (a British tribe based in East Anglia) led a rebellion against Roman rule. Within a very short time the insurgents attacked and burnt Colchester, London and St Albans before the Romans recalled their forces and destroyed Boudicca's army. Enfield would undoubtedly have been in the area under the control of the insurgents during the rebellion.

The Roman road from London to York (Ermine Street) crossed Enfield from north to south. From

Bishopsgate to the northern end of Tottenham its line can still be followed in present day roads and from Maidens Bridge northwards it can be traced along Bulls Cross and through Theobalds Park. Between the Tottenham / Edmonton boundary and Maidens Bridge the road has been lost. In Edmonton, Victoria Road, formerly Hyde Lane, must be on or close to the suspected alignment and the rather strange configuration of Bury Street (close to the junction with the A10) may well be the spot where Ermine Street once crossed. The Breton Estate Map of 1785 clearly shows the line of the road preserved in field boundaries running in a north-westerly direction from Lincoln Road towards Bulls Cross, and the very pronounced kink in Lincoln Road, close to the junction with Main Avenue, indicates where Ermine Street intersected.

A Roman settlement grew up in the Bush Hill Park area close to the road. Extensive Roman remains came to light in the area between Main Avenue and Lincoln Road during the 1970s. More Roman material has been discovered in keyhole excavations in back gardens, especially in Landseer Road. A short distance to the south at Churchfield, in the Latymer Road / Bury Street area of Edmonton, Roman remains have been discovered at various dates between 1929 and 1971.

The end of the Roman occupation and its immediate aftermath is still shrouded in mystery. In AD410 the last Roman troops were withdrawn from Britain by the Emperor Honorius, as Rome itself came under threat from the Barbarian hordes that had invaded the Empire. But in AD429 and again in AD448 Germanus, Bishop of Auxerre came to Britain and among the places he visited were London and St Albans. Both cities were clearly still functioning, if only at a reduced level.

THE ANGLO-SAXONS

The Saxon invasions appear to have started in earnest by AD449 with the landing of a major force in Kent. In AD457 the Battle of Crayford left the invaders in full control of Kent, but progress northwards was slow. Only after the battle of Bedford in AD571, a decisive Saxon victory, can it be certain that the Britons finally lost control of London and the north side of the Thames.

Whether Middlesex, as its name suggests, ever formed a separate Saxon kingdom, is far from certain and it is even possible that the territory of the Middle Saxons may at one time have included Surrey as well. But it is clear that Middlesex soon came under the sway of the East Saxons who established their capital alongside the ruins of Roman London.

The process of unifying the separate Anglo-Saxon kingdoms into a single state was a protracted

business with first Northumbria, then Mercia, and finally Wessex gaining the ascendancy. The biggest challenge faced by the newly united state came from the Danish invasions. For a brief spell during the winter of 894/5, the River Lee formed the front line in King Alfred's war against the Danes. In the autumn of 894 a Danish invasion force, which had established a temporary base on Mersea island, Essex, sailed up the Thames and the Lee to a point about twenty miles north of London, which is thought to have been Ware in Hertfordshire. Alfred's forces responded by building two forts beside the river, downstream of the Danish camp, and placing obstructions in the river bed, forcing the Danes to abandon their ships and escape overland.

The death of the Saxon king, Ethelred the Unready, in 1016 threw an already demoralised country into confusion. Edmund Ironside, son of Ethelred, proclaimed king by the English, fought desperately to repel the overwhelming Danish forces under Cnut. In the summer of that year Cnut's army, then engaged in a protracted siege of London, was subject to a surprise attack by Edmund Ironside who led his soldiers through dense woodlands to the north of London. The site of the battle, for long unknown, was identified by the late Sir Frank Stenton, using place-name evidence, as Clay Hill, Tottenham (now Devonshire Hill).

THE CONQUEST AND DOMESDAY

At the time of the Norman Conquest of 1066, Enfield and Edmonton were both held by Ansgar, a nobleman of Anglo-Danish extraction, who held property in seven counties. He was the grandson of Tovi the Proud, a close associate of Cnut, best known today as the founder of the collegiate church that subsequently became Waltham Abbey. It was at Tovi's wedding feast in June 1042 that Harthacnut, the last survivor of Cnut's sons, collapsed and died, thus paving the way for the restoration of the English royal house in the person of Edward the Confessor, son of Ethelred the Unready and brother of Edmund Ironside. Ansgar, who had been a prominent member of the court of Edward the Confessor as well as Sheriff of London and Middlesex, is known to have been wounded at the Battle of Hastings and to have attempted an improvised defence of London. His subsequent fate is uncertain, but he is believed to have died in prison.

Ansgar's lands were given to Geoffrey de Mandeville - who still held Enfield at the time of Domesday Survey (1086). The Enfield entry records the presence of a priest suggesting that there must have been a church probably on the site of the

3. A late 18th-century view of one wing of the Manor House. Much of the building was of timber-framed construction.

present St Andrew's Church in Enfield Town. The earliest part of the existing building dates from the thirteenth century, but the choice of dedication suggests a much older foundation.

There was arable land and meadow for 24 plough teams. There was woodland sufficient to sustain 2000 pigs, exactly the same number as recorded in Edmonton, suggesting that the woodland that subsequently became Enfield Chase, may already have been managed in common by the two parishes. (Nearby Tottenham had only sufficient woodland for 500 pigs.) A mill is recorded, possibly on or near the site of the present Ponders End Mill. There is also mention of fishponds, possibly on Enfield Chase.

Enfield was valued at £50, the same as in the reign of King Edward. However, its value when acquired by de Mandeville is given as £20, which indicates that Enfield may have suffered damage at the time of the Conquest but had recovered in the intervening twenty years. Similarly, Edmonton had been valued at £50 in the reign of King Edward, slumping to £20 immediately after the Conquest, but recovering its full value by 1086. Readers wishing to know more about this period should consult Dr Stephen Doree's excellent paper *Domesday Book and the origins of the Edmonton Hundred* (Edmonton Hundred Historical Society, 1986).

Opposite the church stood the Manor House, which is known to have had a gatehouse and a barn and dovecot standing in its grounds. After 1419 the manor was held by the Duchy of Lancaster and the house was normally let on lease to tenants. By the late sixteenth century, the house was a large E-plan building standing in seven acres of land with barns, stables and orchards. At some time the building became known locally as the 'Palace', a name which caught the public imagination and proved difficult to dislodge, particularly as Queen Elizabeth I stayed there briefly in August 1587 during the period of Henry Middlemore's tenancy. During the late seventeenth century the building housed a boys' boarding school run by Dr Robert Uvedale. Towards the end of the eighteenth century it was in poor repair and all but one wing was demolished. The remaining portion was used successively as a boarding school, a Post Office and as the first home of the Enfield Town Constitutional Club. The building was finally demolished in 1928 to make way for a new building for Pearson's department store. Also destroyed was a magnificent cedar of Lebanon planted by Dr Uvedale. Luckily one room was carefully dismantled by the Leggatt brothers and carefully reassembled in a specially built extension to their home at no.5 Gentleman's Row

ORIGINS OF ENFIELD CHASE

The large area of woodland in the north-west corner of Enfield had by 1136 been transformed by the de Mandeville family into Enfield Chase, a semi-private hunting ground. It was later under the control of the de Bohun family, who succeeded the de Mandevilles as lords of the Manor of Enfield. When that family's male line became extinct, the Chase was inherited by King Henry V. (Henry's father, Henry Bolingbroke, Duke of Lancaster, who became Henry IV on the overthrow of Richard II in 1399, had married Mary de Bohun.) The Chase was to remain Duchy of Lancaster property until the enclosure of 1777. Indeed, the Duchy connection did not cease entirely even then – the Duchy retained the freehold of some properties in the Hadley Wood and Cockfosters areas until very recent times.

Common rights over the Chase were enjoyed by the people of Enfield. These included the rights to graze cattle, to gather firewood and, in the autumn, to drive pigs on to the Chase to feed on acorns and beech mast. (Acorns do not figure prominently in the diet of pigs today – the high tannin content gives the meat a strong flavour, not greatly appreciated by modern palates.) The grazing rights were shared by the adjoining parishes of Edmonton, Monken Hadley and South Mimms, all three in the Edmonton Hundred of Middlesex, suggesting close links probably dating from well before the Conquest. Significantly, Northaw and Cheshunt, both in Hertfordshire, despite having borders closely contiguous with Enfield Chase, enjoyed no such rights.

The Chase also contributed to the local economy in other less legitimate ways. Poaching the king's deer became a major cottage industry in and around Enfield – in many cases, the worst offenders were the keepers who were supposed to be preventing it. The roads to the north of Enfield, which crossed the Chase, became the haunt of criminals, who waylaid and robbed unwary travellers.

THE RIVER LEE

The River Lee rises at Luton and joins the Thames at Bow Creek and in its natural state was more or less navigable as far upstream as Ware and Hertford. In medieval times much of London's grain supply was carried by barge down the Lee and other cargoes must have been moved by this means. The older churches in this locality – St Andrew, Enfield, All Saints, Edmonton and All Hallows, Tottenham – were constructed mainly of Kentish ragstone, derived from quarries in the Maidstone area. The only way that building stone could have reached Enfield is by barge up the Lee.

Navigation of the Lee, particularly in the upper reaches, was fraught with problems. Dry summers could cause a dramatic fall in water levels, resulting in a temporary suspension of barge traffic and there were frequent altercations, some violent, between bargemen and millers, both of whom thought they had a prior claim to the water.

The first serious attempt to improve the navigation came in 1190, when the Abbot of Waltham straightened its course at Waltham Abbey. An Act of Parliament of 1425 was passed to improve navigation between London and Hertford, and appoint commissioners to deal with obstructions caused by fishing weirs and mills. A further Act was passed in 1571 to improving navigation between London and Ware. The river was scoured and in places embanked and straightened. At Waltham a lock was built, one of the first pound locks in the country.

These improvements were not greatly appreciated in Enfield where there were many wealthy

4. The Eleanor Cross at Waltham Cross as it appeared in 1721. It has since undergone several drastic restorations (see p.12).

maltmen, who made a very good living buying malt in Hertfordshire and selling it (with a substantial mark-up) to the London brewers, having transported it there by packhorse. Easier sailing on the River Lee meant that malt could be transported by barge direct from Ware and Hertford to London, thereby cutting out the Enfield middlemen. The resulting unrest came to a head in 1581 in what appears to have been an organised campaign of sabotage. There were attempts to cut the banks of the river near Green Street and to destroy the lock at Waltham.

QUEEN ELEANOR'S LAST JOURNEY

In 1290 Enfield witnessed the funeral procession of Queen Eleanor of Castile, wife of King Edward I. She died at Harby, Nottinghamshire while travelling north to join the king, who was engaged in military operations in Scotland. Her body was brought back for burial at Westminster Abbey (where the tomb can still be seen) and ornamental crosses were later erected at each overnight stop on this journey. The Eleanor Cross at Waltham Cross (much restored) is one of these (see ill.4).

BLACK DEATH AND AFTER

The Black Death struck Enfield late in 1349. An inquisition taken at the Manor of Durants in July of that year reveals no sign of the plague and, apart from a slight decline in land values, possibly due to over-cropping, nothing was apparently amiss. But, by December Enfield had been devastated. At the Manor of Worcesters there were sixty acres of land vacant, where the tenant had died and no heir could be found, strongly suggesting that whole families had been wiped out. A second wave of plague struck Enfield in 1362.

The resulting labour shortage produced wage inflation which the government tried to restrict by legislation, thereby provoking resistance. In July 1351 the king's justices in session at Tottenham were attacked by a mob, which freed all the prisoners, the justices fleeing for their lives.

Evidence for Enfield's participation in the Peasants' Revolt of 1381 is lacking, but there was much activity in neighbouring counties. In Hertfordshire, there was an insurrection at St Albans, where the Abbey (always unpopular) was attacked. (The present gatehouse at St Albans Abbey, built soon after this time, was intended to deter further attacks.) There was violence at Barnet, and at Hertford the castle was attacked and its wine cellars ransacked. In Essex, Brentwood was a hotbed of insurrection and there was trouble at Waltham where the Abbey came under attack. With incidents as close as Barnet and Waltham Abbey, it is very unlikely that Enfield remained unaffected.

WARS OF THE ROSES

The following century saw the protracted civil war known as the Wars of the Roses in which three major battles were fought to the north of London. St Albans, strategically placed on Watling Street, was the site of two major encounters. The first (1455), on the outskirts of the town, resulted in a Yorkist victory. The second (1461) was fought through the streets with victory going to the Lancastrian forces. Closer to Enfield was the Battle of Barnet, fought on the edge of Enfield Chase near the village of Monken Hadley on Easter Sunday, 1471. Yorkist forces, under the command of King Edward IV, advancing from London, engaged a Lancastrian army, led by the Earl of Warwick ('The Kingmaker') advancing from the north. The encounter was a confused and bloody affair, fought in and out of the woodlands of Enfield Chase in thick fog ending in an overwhelming Yorkist victory. Warwick was killed on the battlefield, and his mutilated remains were exhibited in London prior to burial. The local impact was considerable with remnants of the Lancastrian forces being hunted down through neighbouring villages.

SIR THOMAS LOVELL AND ELSING

The victory of Henry VII at Bosworth in 1485 brought the Tudor dynasty to power, resulting in a long period of relative stability. Sir Thomas Lovell, a leading figure in the government of Henry VII and also in the early years of the reign of Henry VIII, was an Enfield resident living at Elsing, a large house at Forty Hill.

Lovell was born *c*.1450, a member of a prominent Norfolk family, long resident at East Harling, near Thetford. (The church at East Harling has monuments to Lovell's nephew and great-nephew.) He was a lawyer by training and was prominent in the affairs of Lincoln's Inn, serving as treasurer and three terms as governor. His political career advanced with the accession of Henry VII. First elected to Parliament in 1485, he served briefly as Speaker of the House of Commons before becoming Chancellor of the Exchequer, an office he held without a break until 1516. Lovell was an astute and wily politician, a loyal and trusted servant of the Tudor dynasty and his record of service can be compared favourably with that of William and Robert Cecil later in the century. In his later years Lovell's influence waned as Cardinal Wolsey's increased and, after losing the Chancellorship, he seems to have largely retired from active politics. He died at Elsing in May 1524, aged about 74, and was buried at Holywell Priory, Shoreditch. Living to a good age and dying of natural causes in his own bed, Lovell's fate must have been envied by many other politicians and courtiers of the sixteenth century, whose careers ended abruptly on the scaffold.

Lovell had inherited Elsing in 1508 through his second wife, Isabel, the daughter of Lord Ros. It had previously belonged to the Tiptoft family – Sir John Tiptoft acquired the property in 1413. A magnificent brass to the memory of Sir John's wife,

5. The brass of Lady Joyce Tiptoft of Elsing in St Andrew's Church. She was the mother of John Tiptoft, Earl of Worcester, known as the 'butcher of England'.

6. The remains of Sir Thomas Lovell's home at Elsing under excavation by the Enfield Archaeological Society in 1964.

Joyce, Lady Tiptoft (died 1446) can still be seen at St Andrew's Church. (Their son, John Tiptoft, Earl of Worcester, a vicious and ruthless man, known as 'the butcher', was a supporter of the Yorkist cause in the Wars of the Roses and was beheaded in 1470 by his Lancastrian opponents. A memorial to him can be seen at Ely Cathedral.)

After Lovell's death, Elsing was inherited by Thomas Manners, Earl of Rutland, who in 1539 was induced to hand the property over to King Henry VIII. (Manners was compensated with some monastic property, including the former Cistercian Abbey of Rievaulx, Yorkshire, of which substantial ruins still survive.) The house was then refurbished and used mainly as accommodation for the royal children, Prince Edward, Princess Mary and Princess Elizabeth. Queen Elizabeth stayed at Elsing in 1564, 1568 and again in 1572. By the end of the sixteenth century the house was becoming increasingly difficult to maintain and, after the acquisition of Theobalds in 1607, Elsing was of no further use to the Crown. It was later occupied by Philip Herbert, Earl of Montgomery who eventually purchased the property from Charles I in 1641 for £5,300. In 1656, Elsing, by now owned by the Rainton family of Forty Hall, was still standing but in an advanced state of dilapidation and was probably demolished soon after. The site (in the meadow between Forty Hall and the Turkey Brook) was partially excavated by the Enfield Archaeological Society 1963/6. (The author, then a teenager, worked on the excavation as a volunteer.)

THE CECILS

One of the most durable political figures in the reign of Elizabeth I was her long-serving Secretary of State and later Lord High Treasurer, William Cecil, Lord Burghley, wise, pragmatic and of unquestionable loyalty. Cecil was a major land-owner in Edmonton, his properties including Pymmes and some large tracts of woodland in Southgate and Winchmore Hill. In 1564 Cecil began building a magnificent country house at Theobalds just north of Enfield in the neighbouring parish of Cheshunt. It was not completed until 1585.

Lord Burghley, as he then was, became involved in Enfield matters when the sorry affair of the Enfield Sunday meat market came to a head in 1585. For some time a Sunday meat market had developed in Enfield Town outside St Andrew's Church. This upset the then Vicar, Leonard Chambers, who understandably resented this threat to both the Sabbath and to his authority. He took every opportunity to denounce this evil and invited learned preachers from Cambridge to bolster his campaign. Finally in 1585 Chambers' patience snapped and, storming out of the church like Christ driving the money changers from the Temple, he and his curate, one Leonard Thickpenny, berated the butchers and overturned one of the stalls, casting the meat upon the ground. This outburst did not have quite the intimidating effect that Chambers must have hoped for. The people of Enfield responded by sending a petition to Burghley in support of the meat market and protesting at the conduct of the Vicar and his curate. It was signed by all but one of the parishioners.

On Burghley's death his office of Secretary of State passed to his younger son, Robert Cecil (later Lord Salisbury) who also inherited Theobalds. Robert, like his father, was a consummate politician, but had none of his father's tact and charm. Hardened by physical disability (he was a hunchback) Cecil junior was a cunning and devious man, ruthless both to rivals and unruly subordinates. He was feared, but not much liked.

In 1603 after the death of Elizabeth, Robert Cecil received at Theobalds James VI of Scotland on his way south to take the throne as James I of England. While Theobalds was being prepared for this most important of guests, the servants were sent into Enfield Chase to gather firewood only to be angrily confronted by a group of Enfield women, who vociferously objected to wood being taken across the border into Cheshunt in blatant violation of their common rights.

James I was a frequent guest of Robert Cecil at Theobalds. On one occasion Cecil staged a lavish entertainment for James I and his visiting brother-in-law, the king of Denmark. The climax was (or should have been) a masque staged in honour of

7. *William Cecil's house at Theobalds, later a royal palace, which was wrecked during the Commonwealth period and, apart from a few fragments in Cedars Park, has largely vanished.*

the two kings, but, owing to the drunken state of the performers, the masque ended in disaster. Somebody tripped and fell, spilling a tray of jelly, spices and cream over the king of Denmark, and, shortly afterwards, other members of the cast made an undignified rush for the door and could be heard vomiting copiously in the courtyard. The performance was abandoned.

In 1607 Theobalds was acquired by the king, Robert Cecil being compensated with the former Bishop of Ely's Palace at Hatfield where most of the former palace was demolished and work commenced on a magnificent new building, Hatfield House, but sadly Robert Cecil died in 1612 and never saw his new home complete. His tomb, a magnificent Jacobean sculpture, can still be seen in the Salisbury Chapel attached to St Ethelreda's Church at Hatfield.

THE MIGHTY WROTHS

Less significant than the Cecils nationally, but more influential locally were the Wroths of Durants Arbour, Ponders End, a large moated manor house that lay to the east of the Hertford Road slightly to the south of today's Enfield College. Durants Arbour had been in the hands of the family since the early fifteenth century. The family also held land elsewhere in Middlesex (especially in Hampstead), in the Epping Forest area of Essex, and in Somerset.

The first of the family to rise to prominence was Robert Wroth I (1488-1535). He was by profession a lawyer, educated at Gray's Inn, retained as counsel by his powerful neighbour, Sir Thomas Lovell of Elsing. He represented Middlesex in the Parliament of 1529 and became Attorney General to the Duchy of Lancaster in 1531. He was a friend of Thomas Cromwell, whose star was then firmly in the ascendant, a relationship that suggests that Wroth was a strong supporter of the Reformation. On his death in 1535, he left his best horse to Thomas Cromwell, who also became guardian of Wroth's eldest son, just eighteen years old at the time of his father's death.

Robert's son, Thomas Wroth (1518-73) also had political aspirations, marrying the daughter of Sir Richard Rich, a one-time associate of Thomas Cromwell, who, as Chancellor of the Court of Augmentations, had played a major part in the disposal of the property of the recently dissolved monasteries. He represented Middlesex in the Parliaments of 1545, 1547, 1553, 1559 and 1563. On the overthrow of Protector Somerset, he became one of the four gentlemen of the privy chamber to the young King Edward VI. His role in the confused events that attended the death of that un-

8. *The Tudor gatehouse at Durants, once the home of the Wroth family.*

happy monarch in 1553 was a decidedly ambiguous one. When the young king was on his deathbed, Wroth was one of the signatories of letters patent drawn up to pass the crown to Lady Jane Grey. (This was designed to prevent the succession of Mary Tudor who, as a Catholic, was regarded, rightly as it turned out, as a threat to the Protestant cause.) Despite this, Wroth, when Jane Grey's cause was clearly lost, deftly switched sides and took part in the proclamation of Mary in July 1553. He thus managed to survive, though clearly regarded by the new regime as highly suspect. In the following year, 1554, Wroth was suspected of complicity in the uprising organised by Henry Grey, Duke of Suffolk, father of Lady Jane. Taking no chances, he fled abroad to Europe, eventually settling in Strasbourg, a city much favoured by English Protestant refugees at this time. After the death of Mary in 1558, he returned to England and resumed his seat in Parliament, but failed to recover his former power and influence.

Thomas' eldest son, Robert Wroth II (1539-1606), had accompanied his father into exile at Strasbourg. He first entered Parliament in 1563 as MP for St Albans, a borough strongly under the influence of the powerful Bacon family. After briefly representing Bossiney in Cornwall, he was elected for Middlesex in 1572 in succession to his father, holding the seat until his death. In 1571 he was primarily responsible for an Act of Parliament for improving the River Lee – this was to have unfortunate repercussions in Enfield (*see p11*). In 1588, at the time of the Spanish Armada he was one of three men placed in charge of the Middlesex trained bands. He also played a major role in the passing of the 1601 Poor Law.

9. An early 19th-century view of Enfield Market Square.

Two younger sons of Thomas Wroth also entered Parliament. John Wroth (dates uncertain) represented Liverpool in 1593, later becoming ambassador to Turkey. Richard Wroth (d.1596) was MP for Appleby in 1571 and for Morpeth in 1572.

Robert's son, Robert Wroth III (1576-1614) first entered Parliament in 1601 for Newtown, Isle of Wight. In 1607, in a by-election following the death of his father, Robert was elected for Middlesex, retaining the seat until his death. He appears to have taken no active role in parliamentary affairs.

Thus ended the Wroth family's involvement in affairs of state. The last Wroth to live at Enfield was Henry, who inherited Durants Arbour in 1642. Showing none of the family's erstwhile political astuteness, Henry backed the losing side in the Civil War and his latter years were bedevilled by debt. On his death in 1671 Durants Arbour was sold. The house was largely destroyed by fire during the eighteenth century, but a Tudor gatehouse managed to survive until 1910. Today the only reminder is the long filled-in moat, which still regularly causes subsidence on the housing estate that now occupies the site.

THE MARKET

In 1619 a grant of a market charter was made to Enfield by King James I and an enlarged Market Place was created by demolishing The Vine public house which stood fronting on Church Street. (The King's Head in the Market Place was probably built to replace it.) The market prospered well into the next century before decline set in. It was still functioning in 1798, but in a very small way and seems to have folded soon afterwards. An attempt to revive it was made in 1826, during the course of which the derelict market house was replaced by a new market cross. This attempt failed but the market was successfully revived late in the nineteenth century.

THE NEW RIVER

By the early seventeenth century, as the Thames became increasingly polluted, London was desperately short of clean drinking water. Hugh Myddelton, a Welshman born at Denbigh, devised a scheme to construct a canal to convey fresh water from springs near Ware to a reservoir on the outskirts of the City at Clerkenwell. The New River, as it was called, was complete by 1613.

The course through Enfield was substantially different from that which it follows today. Then as now, it entered Enfield from Cheshunt, passing under Bullsmoor Lane and Turkey Street. From this point the course swung westwards, passing under Bulls Cross, where the remains of the bridge

10. The former timber aqueduct at Bush Hill, replaced by the present embankment in the mid 1780s.

11. Sir Hugh Myddelton, the promoter of the New River.

can still be seen, and through the grounds of Bowling Green House (now Myddelton House). From here it ran parallel to the Turkey Brook to a point just west of Flash Lane where it crossed the brook and promptly changed direction, running eastwards along the opposite side of the valley. Substantial remains, much of it still holding water, can still be seen in the Whitewebbs Estate and Gough Park.

Emerging from Gough Park, the New River passed under Forty Hill immediately north of the junction with Clay Hill and Baker Street and ran along the northern edge of Ansell's Green now occupied by Myddelton Avenue. Beyond this point the course has been totally obliterated by housing on the Willow Estate developed in the 1930s. Running in a south-easterly direction, passing close to the present day line of Eastbury Avenue and Carisbrooke Close, it eventually rejoined the present course at a point immediately north of the foot-bridge that now links Tenniswood Road to Ladysmith Road. (The present course between Turkey Street and Tenniswood Road was constructed around 1859 and the former loop was then abandoned.) From this point the river runs southwards, eventually swinging due west alongside Nags Head Lane (Southbury Road) and circling around Enfield Town in a wide loop, passing under

12. *The Clarendon Arch which carried Salmons Brook beneath the Bush Hill aqueduct. It survives today in a precarious state as a flood relief channel.*

Silver Street and Church Street and along the edge of what is now the Town Park, before crossing the Edmonton border at Bush Hill. The Enfield Town Loop has now been bypassed by a line of underground cast iron mains running between Southbury Road and Bush Hill. However, apart from two short stretches at Bush Hill and behind Silver Street which have been filled in, most of the loop has been retained for ornamental purposes. In recent years the loop has become badly silted up and plans are currently being devised to deal with this.

RAINTON AND FORTY HALL

Enfield's most prominent citizen in the first half of the seventeenth century was Sir Nicholas Rainton, a native of Lincolnshire, born in 1569. He settled in London, building up a prosperous business, originally in Lombard Street and later in Cornhill, where he traded in expensive silks, taffetas and velvets imported from Italy. He rose rapidly through the ranks of the Haberdashers' Company and in 1621 he became an Alderman of the City of London, representing Aldgate Ward. In 1632 he was elected Lord Mayor and was knighted soon after the expiry of his term of office.

13. *Sir Nicholas Rainton (portrait at Forty Hall).*

14. *Sir Nicholas Rainton's house, Forty Hall.*

He had a house in Enfield as early as 1620, for his name appears in a book from that year listing persons renting pews at St Andrew's Church. Where he was living is uncertain, but a strong candidate must be the property in Forty Hill now known as the Dower House. Although large, it was clearly too small for a man of Rainton's wealth and status. Between 1629 and 1632, on an adjoining site, he built Forty Hall, a magnificent house with adjoining stable block and farm buildings. Luckily, the house has survived intact and still retains plaster ceilings, fireplaces and panelling from Rainton's time.

Rainton was a staunch Puritan and, as such, found himself increasingly at odds with King Charles I as events moved inexorably towards the outbreak of Civil War. In 1640 the King, increasingly desperate for money as a result of his policy of trying to impose bishops and a prayer book on the Church of Scotland, which had led to the disastrous Bishops' War, tried to raise funds from the City of London by means of a forced loan. Rainton not only refused the King's request for cash, but declined to divulge details of the finances of other City men. For this, he and four other aldermen found themselves in the Marshalsea Prison. However, popular demonstrations in support of the prisoners were such that all five were released after just five days. In 1642, after the outbreak of the Civil War, Rainton was offered a seat on the City's Committee of Safety, but politely declined. Whether this was due to infirmity (he was 73) or for other reasons is far from clear, but from this time his involvement in City politics declined and he spent more and more time at Enfield. It was at Forty Hall that he died in 1646, having outlived his wife, children and grandchildren. He was buried at St Andrew's Church, where his magnificent memorial can still be seen. Forty Hall passed to a nephew, Nicholas Rainton junior.

CIVIL WAR AND COMMONWEALTH

As the Civil War drew closer, Rainton's views appear to have been shared by a large number of Enfield people. Attempts to collect Ship Money and Coat and Conduct Money met with claims of poverty or an outright refusal to pay. Many of the same people were later to pay considerably higher sums in taxes levied by Parliament, apparently without complaint.

When Civil War broke out in the summer of 1642, London and the Home Counties came firmly under the control of Parliament. Middlesex, together with Hertfordshire, Essex, Norfolk, Suffolk and Cambridgeshire was overwhelmingly Parliamentary in sympathy. Royalist activity in Sussex and Kent was decisively stamped upon, giving the Parliamentary side control of eastern and southeast England. This, combined with the almost total defection of the Navy to Parliament, was in the longer term to prove fatal to the Royalist cause.

The first clash of arms took place at Edgehill, Warwickshire, on 23 October, 1642, when the King's army marching south met Parliamentary forces under the Earl of Essex, advancing from London. The battle was bloody and indecisive, but the King was able to continue his advance on London, taking Banbury and Oxford, which was to become the Royalist capital for the duration of the war. Approaching London from Reading via Egham, Royalist forces under Prince Rupert reached Brentford on 12 November, fighting a brisk battle with Parliamentary troops through the streets of the town. Rupert's victorious men subsequently went on an orgy of looting and destruction, which was long remembered. Further advance was blocked by Essex's army, backed up by the London Trained Bands, assembled at Turnham Green. Rather than face a battle, Rupert's army retreated to Oxford. No Royalist forces were ever again to get close to London.

News of the outrages at Brentford sent shock waves around the county of Middlesex and in all churches, including Enfield, collections were made for the people of that unhappy town. In case the Royalists should make another attempt on London, Parliamentary soldiers were stationed in Enfield, Edmonton and Tottenham. Their commander, Colonel Richard Browne, was to play a prominent part in the siege of Oxford in 1645.

In 1645 the war entered a decisive phase, with the superior morale and discipline of the Parliamentary forces at last beginning to tell. On 13 June, the King suffered a crushing defeat at Naseby from which he was never to recover. In May the following year, the King surrendered to the Scots, only to be handed over to Parliament, ultimately to be tried and executed.

15. *The Winchmore Hill Friends' Meeting House. The meeting house at Enfield had closed by 1794.*

The Church of England suffered as the puritans gained the upper hand. In Enfield, Dr William Roberts, vicar since 1616, was ejected in 1642, a fate shared by William Muffett, vicar of Edmonton, and also by the vicars of South Mimms and Monken Hadley. The radical doctrines of such sects as the Levellers were increasingly influential in the locality. By 1650 a colony of Diggers, a sect which claimed the right to seize and cultivate common land, had entrenched themselves on Enfield Chase. The Quakers, founded by George Fox, an itinerant preacher from Leicestershire, also established themselves in Enfield.

In 1649, after the King's execution, the palace of Theobalds and its estate was sold off to former Parliamentary soldiers. The once magnificent house was wrecked beyond hope of recovery and today only a few incoherent fragments remain.

In 1656 Parliament authorised an even bigger sell-off: Enfield Chase. After a survey in 1658, sections of the Chase were allocated to Enfield, Edmonton, Hadley and South Mimms for use as common land in lieu of lost grazing rights, but the rest was offered for sale. The purchasers were mainly army officers who set to work quickly

clearing, fencing and ditching their new farms.

All this was greatly resented by the commoners who, accustomed to grazing rights over the whole of the Chase, claimed that the commons were now too small. Relations between the townspeople and soldiers were soon to deteriorate even further. In June 1659 resentment boiled over and hedges and fences were broken down and cattle driven onto the fields of growing crops. The farmers on the Chase responded by hiring soldiers to protect them. Sheep and cattle belonging to the commoners were shot and killed and, on one occasion, a group of soldiers rampaged through Enfield Town, daring the inhabitants to come out and fight. The climax came on 10 July, 1659 when a group of soldiers clashed with a party of local people. Two Enfield men and one woman died in the encounter, but ten wounded soldiers and a sergeant were taken prisoner by the townsfolk. These men were brought before a local magistrate, who had no hesitation in committing them to Newgate.

The resolution of the problem came from outside. In the following year, General George Monck, despairing of the anarchy into which the country had lapsed following the death of Oliver Cromwell,

16. Title page from a contemporary pamphlet describing the disturbances on Enfield Chase in 1659.

took the momentous step of inviting the King to return from exile on the continent. In May 1660, Charles II entered London and the Commonwealth was dead. The Chase at a stroke reverted to a royal hunting ground and Monck found himself ennobled by a grateful monarch as Duke of Albermarle and among the estates granted to him were Theobalds and Old Park.

NONCONFORMISTS

The passing of the Act of Uniformity in 1662 and the issuing of a new Book of Common Prayer, saw the Church of England reinstated as the national church. A series of Acts, collectively called the Clarendon Code, sought to bolster the Church's authority, but they also had the effect of polarising and strengthening opposition sects. Ministers were required to take an Oath of Uniformity or face ejection. Daniel Manning, the then minister of Enfield, a Presbyterian, felt unable to conform and was duly expelled.

Within a short time of the Restoration, there is evidence of at least three Presbyterian ministers active in Enfield. By 1669 a short-lived Baptist congregation was established. In 1689 its Baker Street Chapel was taken over by a Presbyterian

congregation under their minister Obadiah Hughes. The site of the chapel is today occupied by a hall belonging to the Enfield Evangelical Free Church, continuing an association with Nonconformity which has so far lasted at least 330 years.

The Quakers, then regarded as the most radical of the nonconformist sects, suffered the worst persecution. An Edmonton magistrate, Joshua Galliard of Bury Hall, was particularly zealous in his pursuit of them. Meetings were broken up and members subject to summary imprisonment, fines and distraints upon their property. Nonetheless, the movement survived and the founder, George Fox, is known to have visited both Enfield and Winchmore Hill. A meeting house was established at Winchmore Hill in 1688 which, rebuilt in 1790, happily survives to this day. Another meeting house at Enfield, set up in a former barn at Baker Street in 1697, closed in 1794. A group of cottages forming a *cul de sac* on the north side of Baker Street, retained the name Meeting House Yard until demolition c.1910.

THE GREAT PLAGUE

Enfield experienced major outbreaks of plague in 1603 and 1625 and smaller outbreaks in 1609/10, 1637 and 1641. Located on a main highway, Enfield was vulnerable to epidemics. In 1665, the year of the Great Plague in London, there were many deaths in Enfield and it is known that some of the dead were buried at places other than the churchyard, thereby giving rise to persistent, but unconfirmed rumours of a plague pit at Chase Green. The George in Enfield Town was particularly hard hit for, within a few days, the landlord saw the deaths of his wife, three of his children and three servants.

ROAD AND RIVER

Road maintenance had been a parish responsibility since the mid-sixteenth century. With limited resources from a highway rate, the parish authorities could keep the local roads in reasonable order, filling in the worst of the pot holes, but the task of maintaining heavily used trunk roads, such as the Old North Road through Enfield, was manifestly beyond them. The fact that the majority of the road users came from outside the parish was hardly an incentive to greater efforts on the part of the parish officials.

A precedent was set in 1663 with the establishment of what later became the Wadesmill Turnpike Trust. This body took over a stretch of the busy Old North Road in Hertfordshire with powers to improve the road and recover the costs from users in the form of tolls. In 1713 an Act of Parliament established the Stamford Hill Turnpike Trust to take over a substantial section of the same road from the northern edge of Shoreditch through to the Middlesex-Hertfordshire boundary at Waltham Cross. The Trust later took over Green Lanes from Newington Green to Enfield Town and some link roads such as Church Street, Edmonton. Standards of road maintenance improved considerably and journey times between Enfield and London were much reduced. The Stamford Hill and Green Lanes Turnpike lasted until 1826 when its powers were transferred to the newly formed Metropolis Turnpike Trust.

The eighteenth century also saw a determined effort to put the navigation of the River Lee on a sound footing. The river had been subject to piecemeal attempts at improvement from medieval times , but with mixed results. An Act of 1766 placed the control of the river into the hands of trustees. Under the supervision of the eminent civil engineer, John Smeaton, a programme of improvements was carried out between Limehouse and Hertford, which included locks and weirs to control the water level. Enfield Lock and Ponders End Lock were both installed at this time and the course through Enfield was straightened. The result was a dramatic improvement in the navigation. As before, large cargoes of grain were carried from Ware and Hertford, much of this being barley destined for east London breweries.

Bulk cargoes, such as coal and timber, now deserted the roads for the river. The usefulness of the Lee Navigation was considerably increased when it was later linked to the Grand Union Canal via the Hertford Union Canal and the Regent's Canal.

THE CANNING CASE

Enfield attained brief prominence in 1754 as a result of the Elizabeth Canning kidnapping case. Early in 1754 Elizabeth Canning an eighteen-year-old servant girl, turned up at her mother's home at Aldermanbury in a dishevelled, and emaciated condition. The girl claimed to have been set upon by two men at Houndsditch who, after robbing her, dragged her several miles to a house, where she had been held against her will and attempts were made to force her into prostitution. She had eventually escaped by prising loose a board covering a first floor window and jumped down to the ground and had then found her way back home.

From Elizabeth's description the place of her imprisonment was identified as Mother Wells' house at Enfield – this was a house of ill repute, formerly a pub which stood on the corner of Ordnance Road and the Hertford Road, opposite the Sun and Woolpack. The house was searched

17. An early 20th-century view of the Lee Navigation at Ponders End.

18. *Elizabeth Canning on trial for perjury.*

and Susannah Wells, Virtue Hall and a gypsy woman called Mary Squires were arrested. They were duly tried and found guilty, but almost immediately doubts were expressed about the evidence and Mary Squires, who had been sentenced to death, was in the event pardoned. There then followed an even more sensational trial in which Elizabeth Canning found herself in the dock accused of perjury. Found guilty, she was sentenced to transportation to the American Colonies. The Canning case remains controversial, having inspired many books over a long period. The truth will probably never be established.

END OF THE CHASE

The final years of Enfield Chase were bedevilled by corrupt officialdom, theft of timber and poaching of the king's deer on a massive scale. In 1775 the Duchy Court decided to enclose the Chase, making proposals that were virtually identical to those implemented under the Commonwealth 120 years previously. Mimms and Hadley were happy to accept what was on offer, but the Enfield Vestry managed to negotiate a considerable increase in the size of its allotment.

The Act for Enclosure was passed in 1777. The allotments granted to Enfield, Edmonton and Hadley were used as parish commons in lieu of lost grazing rights. (The Hadley Allotment, managed by a board of trustees, remains common land to this day and is one of the few substantial tracts

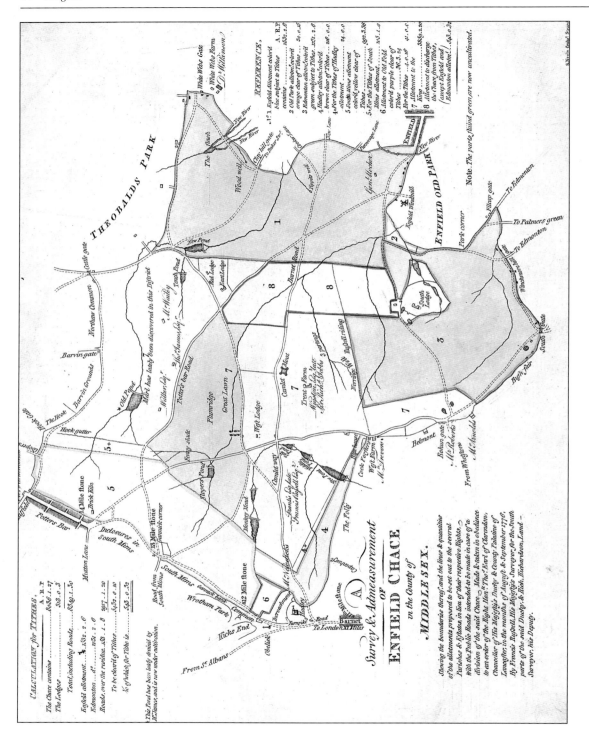

19. *Enfield Chase enclosure map of 1777.*

20. *An early 19th-century view of Trent Park, built for the royal physician, Sir Richard Jebb.*

of Enfield Chase to retain its original vegetation.) The South Mimms allotment was immediately enclosed and parcelled out among the existing landowners of the parish.

Edmonton and Enfield continued using their allotments as common grazing for another twenty-five years or so. Then both parishes were enclosed (Edmonton in 1801 and Enfield 1803) and in both cases the Chase Allotments were divided up among existing landowners and those parishioners who could prove common rights.

The remaining portion of the Chase was divided up by the Duchy of Lancaster into plots on long leases. A large tract, consisting of three plots, was acquired by the royal physician, Sir Richard Jebb, who built himself a small hunting lodge. This building, now much enlarged, forms the core of the mansion at Trent Park.

Another large portion of land was acquired by Francis Russell, a Duchy of Lancaster surveyor, who built himself a large house which, with becoming modesty, he called Russell Mansion; he lived there until his death in 1795. Later known as Beech Hill Park, the house survives as the clubhouse of the prestigious Hadley Wood Golf Club.

For many of the people who purchased portions of the Chase, the land was not quite the bargain it appeared to be. The land had to be cleared, drained, hedged and ditched at considerable labour and expense, and the soil consisted mainly of a heavy clay which proved to be singularly resistant to the agricultural methods of the time.

21. *Francis Russell, a Duchy of Lancaster surveyor, who managed to acquire Beech Hill Park.*

22. *Francis Russell's house at Beech Hill Park, now the home of Hadley Wood Golf Club.*

WILKES AND LIBERTY

Enfield, together with the other parishes of Middlesex, found itself caught up in the meteoric political career of John Wilkes. Wilkes was born in 1725 in Clerkenwell, the son of Israel Wilkes, a wealthy gin distiller. His mother, Sarah, owned property in Enfield at Parsonage Lane and his younger brother, Heaton Wilkes, who took over the family business, also owned property in Enfield.

John Wilkes's political career began in 1757, when he entered the Commons in a by-election as one of the MPs for Aylesbury. He was then a supporter of the faction within the Whig party led by William Pitt the Elder and his brothers-in-law, George Grenville and Earl Temple. When George III acceded to the throne in 1760 he was determined on a decisive change of policy and managed to force the resignations, first of Pitt as Secretary of State, and then of the Prime Minister, the Duke of Newcastle. The new Prime Minister was the Earl of Bute, a Scottish nobleman, favourite and one-time tutor to the new king.

Wilkes found himself in opposition for the first time and discovered a new talent for journalism. He founded the *North Briton*, a satirical journal in which he attacked with devastating effect the King and his unpopular Prime Minister. The campaign culminated in 1763 in issue no. 45 in which Wilkes attacked the King's speech with studied insolence. The government, stung into action, responded by arresting Wilkes on a general warrant (in which no persons were named) and seizing all copies of the offending issue. Wilkes fought back through the courts, winning a stunning victory in which general warrants were declared illegal, but the confiscated copies of no. 45 were ordered to be burnt outside the Royal Exchange by the common hangman. However, when in December 1763 that official tried to carry out the sentence, he found himself within minutes surrounded by a very large and hostile crowd and withdrew hastily after being pelted with mud and other missiles. The Lord Mayor, William Bridgen, and other City officials very pointedly made no effort to intervene. (Bridgen had a country house, Bridgen Hall, at Enfield. This property, now flats, still stands at the junction of Russell Road and Hallside Road.)

Soon after this, Wilkes was injured in a duel and, with his enemies closing in on him, fled to France, where he was to remain in exile for four years. In his absence he was declared an outlaw and ex-

23. *The formidable John Wilkes.*

pelled from Parliament. Early in 1768, with a general election imminent, Wilkes returned and stood unsuccessfully for the City of London. Unperturbed, he immediately offered himself as a candidate for one of the two county seats for Middlesex. Wilkes had good connections in the county both through the family business in Clerkenwell and property at Enfield. Several of his strongest allies on the City Corporation had involvement in the Enfield area and were able to influence the voters. Apart from Bridgen, Alderman James Townsend, who was also MP for West Looe, owned Bruce Castle at Tottenham; Alderman John Sawbridge, MP for Hythe, was a landowner in Tottenham and Edmonton; Alderman Barlow Trecothick, a City MP and Wilkes sympathiser, held a long lease of East Lodge on Enfield Chase. At the election Wilkes was elected defeating the government supporter, Sir William Beauchamp Proctor, having won a clear majority of votes cast in Enfield, Edmonton and Tottenham.

However, there was still the matter of outlawry, for which, despite the cry of 'Wilkes and Liberty' by the London mob, he was imprisoned for 22 months in the King's Bench Prison. The government then expelled Wilkes from the House and, in the by-election that followed in April 1769, with his nomination proposed by Townsend and seconded by Sawbridge, he stood again and was overwhelmingly re-elected with strong support in

24. *Bridgen Hall, the Enfield home of Wilkes' supporter, Alderman William Bridgen. The house, now crudely divided into flats, stands at the junction of Hallside Road and Russell Road.*

25. Enfield Market showing the King's Head (left) where Sir Francis Burdett was entertained to dinner by his supporters. Two people were crushed to death as his coach was drawn in triumph through the town.

Enfield and district. He was expelled from the House yet again and the government took the unusual step of allowing his defeated opponent, Colonel Henry Luttrell to take the seat.

Denied a seat in Parliament, Wilkes became a City Alderman and consolidated his power base, eventually becoming Lord Mayor in 1774. His greatest triumph came in 1771 when he came into conflict with the government over the right of newspapers to publish reports of parliamentary debates, hitherto regarded as a breach of privilege. By deliberately publishing reports in his newspaper, the *Middlesex Journal*, he provoked the government into action. A botched attempt to arrest the printers and publishers developed into a clash between government and the City of London, culminating in the humiliation of Parliamentary officials. Wilkes was triumphantly re-elected for Middlesex in 1774 and this time there was no attempt to expel him. He was to represent Middlesex until he retired from the House in 1790, but by this time his radicalism had cooled and he achieved little in his latter years.

BURDETT AND NO BASTILLE

The general election of 1802 saw another radical upsurge in Middlesex with the election of Sir Francis Burdett, the darling of the London mob. The streets this time rang to the cry of 'Burdett and no Bastille'. The poll at Brentford was both protracted and violent and Burdett's victory was ultimately clinched by a large contingent of voters from Enfield, Edmonton and Tottenham. Shortly after Burdett's supporters gave a dinner in his honour at the King's Head in Enfield Town. A large and eager crowd turned out to see their hero and he sat down to dinner with 200 supporters who had paid seven shillings a head for the privilege. Free drink was distributed to the crowds outside, who later triumphantly drew Burdett in his coach through the Town and Chase Side. During the course of this two men were run over and fatally injured. After Burdett's departure, the mood of the crowd turned ugly, as it rampaged through the King's Head, smashing glasses and crockery.

Burdett's radicalism mellowed as he got older. His latter years in Parliament, after the 1832 Reform Act, were spent as Conservative MP for North Wiltshire. The young Benjamin Disraeli, who knew him at the end of his career, commented aptly: 'He was looked upon as a Jacobin, when in reality he was a Jacobite'.

Enfield 1803

ENCLOSURE

The Enfield Enclosure Act of 1803 and its accompanying award and map give a remarkably detailed picture of the parish at the dawn of the nineteenth century.

The purpose of enclosure was to improve agriculture by abolishing the medieval system of open field cultivation in which land was allocated in small strips to different farmers. Instead, it aimed to rearrange the strips in compact holdings. The cause of agricultural improvement took on a special urgency from the Revolutionary and Napoleonic Wars which resulted in a drastic decrease in grain imports and it was therefore vital to maximise food production. Many Middlesex and Hertfordshire parishes opted for enclosure around this time: Cheshunt (1799), Edmonton (1801), Finchley (1810) and Hornsey (1812).

A group of Enfield gentry led by Sir George Prescott, William Mellish and Newell Connop, organised a petition for enclosure among the larger landowners. This was favourably received by Parliament and a Bill was quickly drafted and presented. A counter-petition from those who stood to lose out was hastily brushed aside, and the Bill rapidly became law.

All common rights were abolished in Enfield. The land in the Enfield Chase Allotment and on the common marshes was distributed among existing landowners and those who could prove entitlement to common rights. That in the open fields was reallocated in holdings, as far as possible close to the owner's home. The allotments given to former holders of common rights were small, of poor quality and were mostly located on the Chase, or on the marshes, remote from the owners' homes. The former commoners were saddled with the expense of fencing and ditching their allotments, which many of them could not afford, thus forcing them to sell. In the enclosure award there are many instances of land changing hands in this fashion *during* the actual enclosure process. One who acquired a considerable acreage in this fashion was Henry Sawyer, a wealthy Enfield Town solicitor, who had been appointed as an enclosure commissioner with the task of overseeing the implementation of the Act. Sawyer was undoubtedly using inside information for personal gain.

Agriculture in Enfield benefited substantially from enclosure and became both more efficient and profitable. But as the big landowners consolidated their hold on the parish, the poor, stripped of

26. A dilapidated barn at Bulls Cross, drawn in 1797 by J.T. Smith.

common rights, found the last buffer between them and parish relief had been removed.

THE ENCLOSURE MAP

The map shows the parish in some detail: The centre of Enfield Town is already well developed and the church, the Market Square and the Town itself with its distinct funnel shape can all be clearly discerned. North of the Town, there is intermittent ribbon development along Silver Street and Baker Street as far as the junction with New Lane (Lancaster Road). To the south and east, London Road and Nags Head Lane (Southbury Road) show little sign of building. Along what had until 1777 been the eastern boundary of the Chase, Gentleman's Row is built and to the north there are signs of sporadic building along the line of Chase Side and Brigadier Hill.

Along the eastern edge are the straight lines of the River Lee cut under Smeaton's supervision some thirty years earlier. The large settlement of Ponders End is distinctly L-shaped with one arm running westwards along South Street from the mill and the Lee to the junction with the High Road, and the other arm northwards along both sides of the High Road as far as Nags Head Lane. On the north side of South Street, Scotland Green already has a few houses. North of Ponders End, the remains of the great moated house of Durants, once the home of the Wroth family, stand slightly to the east of the High Road.

To the north is Enfield Highway, an elongated settlement strung out along the Hertford Road from Green Street as far as Hoe Lane. South of

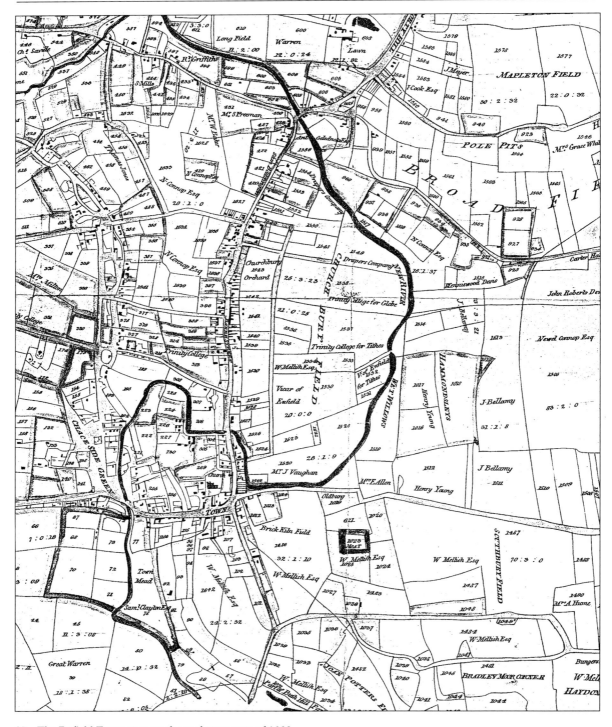

27. The Enfield Town area on the enclosure map of 1803.

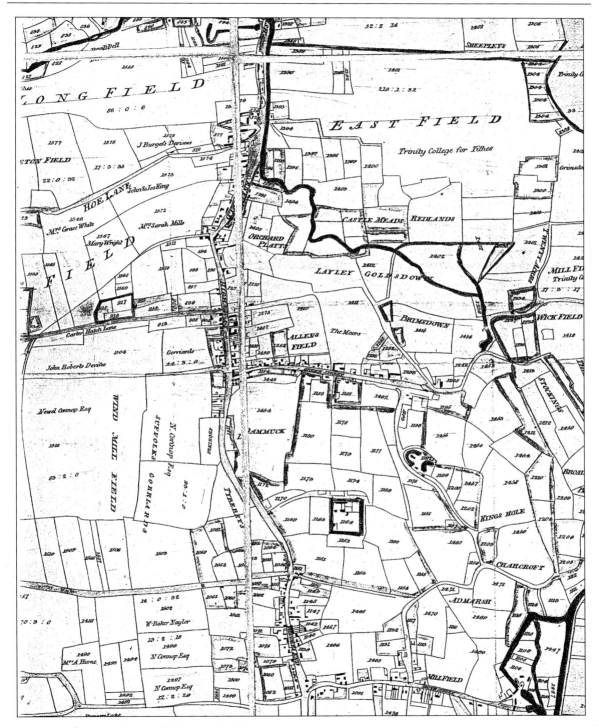

28. *Ponders End and Enfield Highway in 1803.*

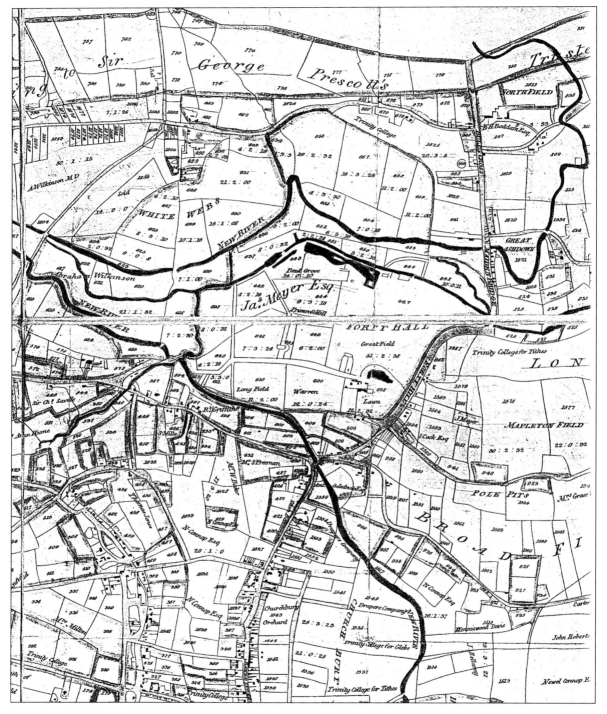

29. *Forty Hill and Bulls Cross in 1803.*

30. A badly decayed timber-framed house at Green Street, drawn in 1797 by J.T. Smith.

Hoe Lane there is a pronounced kink in the road, even then a source of traffic congestion. This was by-passed in 1832 when the road here was straightened. (The former main road survives as Old Road and Pitfield Way.) Green Street, once a self-contained settlement, is on the map now firmly linked to Enfield Highway.

Enfield Wash then consisted of ribbon development along the Hertford Road either side of the Turkey Brook. The map shows a bridge standing slightly to the west of the present bridge. This was a wooden structure erected by the Stamford Hill Turnpike Trust in 1772, which by 1814 was in a decidedly dangerous condition. It was replaced in 1821 by a timber bridge, which sufficed until it was replaced by the present brick Woolpack Bridge. To the west, there is scattered development along Turkey Street almost as far as Bulls Cross.

THE RURAL FRINGE
To the north of Enfield Town is Forty Hill, a settlement centred on Forty Hill Green. From this development projects northwards along Forty Hill itself. Immediately north of Maidens Bridge is Bulls Cross consisting of a group of cottages between the bridge and the Turkey Street junction and another group of cottages facing into Bullsmoor Lane. There are also two tiny outlying settlements: Bridge Street, located in Clay Hill, and Romey Street, in Whitewebbs Lane.

LANES AND TURNPIKES
Most of the roads on the map, albeit in many cases with altered names, have survived to this day. Indeed much of the pattern of modern Enfield is already established.

South of Enfield Town, the main road, then as now, is London Road, usually known as London Lane. Before the upgrading of Village Road and Park Avenue to take tram tracks (1909), the main road ran over the top of Bush Hill. Leading east from London Road to Ponders End was what was then known as Brick Kiln Lane, renamed Lincoln Road in 1888. This road was known variously as Bungey Lane, Brickfield Lane, Red Lane and Joan Potters Lane.

Leading east from the Town is Nags Head Lane, so called from the former pub of that name. This had originally been a minor road giving access to the great open fields that lay between Ponders End and the Town. It continued eastwards as a footpath, linking up with Farm Lane a similar thoroughfare running west from Ponders End. Under the terms of the Enclosure Act the footpath was upgraded, thus making a through road, which was known as Nags Head Lane until renamed Southbury Road in 1882.

North of the Town, Silver Street (continued as Baker Street) is the main link with Forty Hill and Bulls Cross and Parsonage Lane leads westwards to Chase Side. On the east side of Baker Street is a small *cul-de-sac*, known as Fighting Cocks Lane from a former public house. This was later extended westwards to Chase Side and renamed Gordon Road. Running parallel with Baker Street is Churchbury Lane, sometimes known as Cherry Orchard Lane, a former field track that had recently been elevated to full highway status.

Leading west from Baker Street towards Lavender Hill and Chase Side is New Lane, renamed Lancaster Road in 1887. It is linked to Clay Hill by Brigadier Hill, Phipps Hatch Lane and Cocker Lane (Browning Road).

Along the old eastern boundary of Enfield Chase ran Chase Side and Gentleman's Row. The latter has changed remarkably little in nearly 200 years and is one of the finest Georgian streets in Middlesex. It can be compared favourably with Chiswick Mall and Harrow-on-the-Hill and is a street of which Enfield can be justly proud. Chase Green, formed from some spare land left over after enclosure, is larger and more irregular in shape than at present. Some land along the western edge was lost when the Great Northern Railway was extended across it in 1910.

On the Chase itself a network of roads is already in place, some being old trackways upgraded, others laid out since enclosure. From the Town the

main exit to the west is Windmill Hill, the eponymous mill surviving until 1904. This linked up with East Barnet Road (Slades Hill) and The Ridgeway. Other roads shown on the Chase include Holtwhites Hill, Lavender Hill, East Lodge Lane, Hadley Road, Cattlegate Road and Theobalds Park Road.

Three roads run east from Forty Hill and Bulls Cross: Carterhatch Lane (sometimes called Potash Lane), Turkey Street and Bullsmoor Lane. Since the enclosure of the Chase, Whitewebbs Lane had been extended from the old Chase boundary to join Theobalds Park Road and Cattlegate Road.

On the eastern side, the great turnpike road (now Ponders End High Street and the Hertford Road) is a prominent feature, running from the Edmonton border north to Waltham Cross. East of this there are roads leading into what had until recently been the common marshes adjoining the Lee. These include Duck Lees Lane, Millmarsh Lane, Stockingswater Lane, Bell Lane and Painters Lane, many of the names reflecting the low-lying and waterlogged nature of the ground. From Enfield Wash, Welches Lane, also known as Lock Lane and Marsh Lane, but better known today as Ordnance Road, runs east to the Lee at Enfield Lock. This fairly insignificant thoroughfare was soon to assume a new importance with the opening of the Royal Small Arms Factory.

31. Gentleman's Row, a remarkable Georgian street that survives largely intact. Some of the houses have earlier timber-framed structures concealed behind 18th-century brickwork.

32. Bush Hill Park, home of William Mellish, then one of the biggest landowners in Edmonton and Enfield.

33. *Old Park on Bush Hill, now the home of the Bush Hill Park Golf Club.*

34. *Chase Side House, which formerly stood on the site of the Library Green.*

PARTICULARS and CONDITIONS of SALE

OF A

Valuable Freehold Eftate,

Confifting of the MANORS of

WORCESTER and GOLDBEATERS,

WITH

COURT BARON, together with all their IMMUNITIES, ROYALTIES, QUIT RENTS, &c.

SPACIOUS MANSION,

Extenfive OFFICES, *Garden, Pleafure Ground*, elegant Green Houfe, Lawn, &c.

PARK of 400 ACRES,

Embellifhed with Wood and Water, and furrounded with a ftrong Oak Pale,

CALLED

FORTY HALL,

SITUATE

At ENFIELD, in the County of *Middlefex*,

LATE THE RESIDENCE AND PROPERTY OF

ELIAB BRETON, Efq; dec.

TOGETHER WITH

Sundry ELIGIBLE FARMS, with their requifite Buildings, containing in the Whole near

ONE THOUSAND EIGHT HUNDRED ACRES,

OF THE ANNUAL VALUE OF

Two Thoufand Six Hundred POUNDS.

WHICH (BY ORDER OF THE EXECUTORS)

Will be *Sold by Auction* by Mr. CHRISTIE,

At his Great Room in PALL MALL,

On *Thurfday* 24th and *Friday* 25th of *May*, 1787,

Beginning at TWELVE o'Clock each Day.

In SIXTY-FIVE LOTS.

The Bailiff attends at the Manfion, who will fhew the Eftate; of whom Particulars may be had; alfo at the *Rainbow Coffee Houfe, Cornbill*, and in *Pall Mall*, where a Plan of the Eftate may be feen.

35. *Title page of the 1787 sale catalogue of Forty Hall.*

THE BIG HOUSES

Enfield had a substantial number of large country houses, mostly occupied by wealthy Londoners. These are readily identifiable on the enclosure map.

On Bush Hill, just inside the Edmonton boundary, stands Bush Hill Park, a substantial house, the home of William Mellish MP. A member of an old established Nottinghamshire family, Mellish was a director of the Bank of England and was Tory MP for one of the Middlesex county seats from 1806 to 1820, having previously been MP for Grimsby. The estate was considerable and straddled the Enfield/Edmonton boundary. Most of the land between Lincoln Road and Bury Street was owned by Mellish. The house survived until 1927.

On the opposite side of Bush Hill, just inside the Enfield boundary, is Old Park, a property built in the centre of a prehistoric earthwork. It had been in the hands of the Clayton family since 1735. In

1809 Rev. T. Winchester Lewis and his young bride, Elizabeth, daughter of Isaac Walker of Arnos Grove, took a lease on the house. In 1826, Elizabeth, by now a widow, purchased the freehold. Her daughter, also called Elizabeth, married Edward Ford of Lancaster, who eventually inherited the property, which remained in the hands of the Ford family until 1909. Old Park is now the club house of the Bush Hill Park Golf Club. Parts of the estate ended up in other hands. Chase Park, home to the Browning family and later to the Carrs, was built in the angle between Windmill Hill and the drive to Old Park (now Old Park Avenue). Chase Side House was built on the south side of Church Street, roughly on the site of the Library Green. Its surviving grounds now form the Town Park.

Forty Hall had just been purchased (1799) by

36. *Whitewebbs House, built in 1791 for Dr Abraham Wilkinson.*

James Meyer, a wealthy merchant of Dutch extraction. The Forty Hall Estate had been sold in 1787 by the family of Eliab Breton, who had acquired it by marriage to Elizabeth Wolstenholme, heiress to the Rainton estates. Much of the outlying lands were dispersed, but Forty Hall and its immediate estate were purchased by Edmund Armstrong who was to enjoy possession for just ten years, dying in 1797. His heirs, pursued by creditors, were forced to sell up in 1799.

Whitewebbs House was built in 1791 by Dr Abraham Wilkinson on land acquired in 1787 on the break up of the Breton Estate. It replaced an earlier house of the same name, on the north side of Whitewebbs Lane, which had been one of the safe houses used by the Gunpowder Plot conspirators in 1605. Wilkinson was an enthusiastic supporter of agricultural improvement and made considerable efforts to raise the standard of cultivation on his estate. The Wilkinson family was to retain the Whitewebbs Estate until 1900.

Capel House (now Capel Manor Horticultural Centre) was owned by Rawson Hart Boddam, a wealthy retired East India Company official, formerly Governor of Bombay. He also owned a considerable amount of land in the Bullsmoor Lane area. The connection with India was revived when the house was later owned by the Warren family whose wealth derived from the tea trade.

A large strip of land along the northern edge of Enfield in the Whitewebbs Lane / Cattlegate Road area formed part of the Theobalds Estate owned by wealthy banker, Sir George Prescott. The bulk of the estate lay across the border in Cheshunt. Prescott's home was the present Theobalds, a large property dating from 1768, built on a different site from the original Tudor house, which lay well to the east.

On the north side of Clay Hill, adjoining the southern entrance to Whitewebbs, stands Clayesmore, then occupied by Mrs Ann Hume. It was subsequently owned by Edward Harman, on whose bankruptcy in 1847 the house was acquired

37. *Capel House (now Capel Manor Horticultural Centre) then the home of Rawson Hart Boddam, a former governor of Bombay.*

38. *The present Theobalds House (not on the site of the original), home of Sir George Prescott, drawn in 1798.*

by the Huguenot banker, James Whatman Bosanquet. His grandson was B.J.T. Bosanquet, the well-known Middlesex and England cricketer, and inventor of the googly. His great grandson, possibly even better known, was the former ITN newsreader, Reginald Bosanquet. At the turn of the century the house was briefly used for a boys' preparatory school run by a young schoolmaster called Alex Devine. This school, after several moves, survives today and, now located at Iwerne Minster in Dorset, still retains the name Clayesmore. The house was demolished in the late 1930s, leaving a lodge house as the only reminder.

On the west side of Bulls Cross is Bowling Green House, the home of Daniel Garnault, a member of another Huguenot family long connected with the New River Company. On his death in 1809, the property passed to his sister Anne, wife of Henry Carrington Bowles, a wealthy publisher and print seller. In 1818 he built himself a new house, Myddelton House, next to the old house which was then demolished. Myddelton House was to remain in the hands of the Bowles family until the death of E.A. (Gussie) Bowles in 1954.

In the south-west angle of Baker Street and Parsonage Lane is Enfield Court, dating at least in part from the late seventeenth century, then owned by Robert Buckworth. It was later acquired by General John Martin, a Waterloo veteran, on whose death in 1852 it passed to his godson, Col. Sir Alfred Somerset, grandson of the fifth Duke of Beaufort and nephew of Crimean War commander, Lord Raglan. After the death of Somerset in 1915, the property was sold to the trustees of Enfield Grammar School and remains in use as the Lower School.

The enclosure map also shows Grove House, which stood in the southern angle between Turkey Street and the Hertford Road. The grounds include an ornamental waterway fed from the Turkey Brook. Grove House is chiefly memorable as the home of Matthew Michell, the wealthy patron of the artist, Thomas Rowlandson. The house was demolished in the 1930s, the lake drained and the site built over.

Durants, once the home of the Wroth family, was now owned by Newell Connop, the biggest land-owner in East Enfield, whose wealth derived from a gin distillery in Shadwell. Another major land-owner in East Enfield was William Baker Naylor, a prosperous coal merchant with extensive land holdings in Ponders End.

39. Myddelton House, Bulls Cross, built for Henry Carrington Bowles in 1818.

40. Enfield Court, Baker Street, home of General John Martin, and then of Sir Alfred Somerset, now used by Enfield Grammar School.

The largest institutional landowner in Enfield, apart from the Duchy of Lancaster's holdings on the former Chase, was Trinity College, Cambridge. This college, founded by Henry VIII, had taken over the endowments of the former Walden Abbey, which included land in Enfield. It held the Rectory Manor, whose manor house stood at the junction of Parsonage Lane and Baker Street on the site now occupied by Monastery Gardens, plus tracts of land scattered across Enfield. These included what was eventually called College Farm, and which survives today as Albany Park. (The former farmhouse still stands adjoining the Albany Swimming Pool.) Trinity College remains to this day patron of St Andrew's Church, retaining the right to nominate the clergy and the majority of past vicars have been Trinity College graduates.

Other institutional landowners included the Drapers' Company who held land in Churchbury Field, in Wildmarsh and on the Chase at Theobalds Park Road. Also, St Bartholomew's Hospital owned land at Wildmarsh and held the freehold of the Red Lion pub at Enfield Highway.

41. *Clayesmore, home of the Enfield branch of the Bosanquet family.*

42. *The Rectory Manor House in Baker Street, the property of Trinity College, Cambridge. The site is now occupied by Monastery Gardens.*

Charles Lamb's Enfield

Charles Lamb (1775-1834), the distinguished essayist, settled permanently in Enfield in 1827. He and his sister, Mary, had been living at Colebrooke Row, Islington, but once Lamb had retired from the East India Company, he decided to move out to rural Enfield. In the autumn of 1827 they moved into a house in Chase Side, later known as The Poplars, which was to be their home for two years. Mary Lamb's deteriorating health and increasingly frequent mental breakdowns forced a change of plan and in September 1829 they moved next door to live as lodgers in the home of Thomas Westwood. Initially Lamb settled in well but, in time, he found Westwood's company irksome. Thus, in May 1833 he made what was to be his last move to Bay Cottage, Church Street, Edmonton, and it was here that he died in December 1834; he was buried nearby in the churchyard of All Saints Church.

Lamb was a prolific letter writer and throughout his time in Enfield he maintained a correspondence with a wide circle of friends. His letters provide a lively, gossipy and, at times, malicious commentary on people and events, and they reveal much about the state of Enfield as it entered the third decade of the nineteenth century.

Enfield was the largest parish in Middlesex with 12,653 acres, its nearest rival being Harrow with 10,027 acres. Its population in 1831 was 8,812, making it one of the most populous parishes in the county. Indeed, of the Middlesex parishes outside the metropolis only one had a population greater than Enfield – Hammersmith with 10,222. Close behind were Hampstead (8,588) and Edmonton (8,192). Despite these figures, a study of the growth-rate of population of Enfield from 1801 to 1831 shows that it was increasing at a slower rate than in Tottenham and Edmonton, a trend that was confirmed in the decade 1841/1851.

By 1851 Edmonton had overtaken Enfield and by 1861 so had Tottenham. It was not until the final decade of the nineteenth century that Enfield's population began to increase rapidly. Thus, at the time of Charles Lamb's residence, Enfield was showing signs of economic and demographic stagnation.

43. Westwood Cottage in Chase Side, Lamb's home 1829-33.

44. Charles Lamb as a young man

ECONOMIC DECLINE

Lamb captured this down-at-heel atmosphere precisely in a letter he wrote to Mary Shelley in January 1830. 'Enfield', he writes, 'is seated most indifferently upon the borders of Middlesex, Essex and Hertfordshire, partaking of the quiet dullness of the first and the total want of interest pervading the two latter counties'. Cultural life, then as now, was somewhat limited: 'The chief bookseller deals in prose versions of the melodrama, with plates of ghosts and murders and other subterranean passages'. For someone who had grown up in central London; the foodstuffs on sale in Enfield were dull: 'The tarts in the only pastry-cook-looking shop are baked stale. The macaroons are perennial, kept torpid in glass cases, excepting when Mrs — gives a card party'. Enfield Town was bad enough, but the outlying districts he found even less to his liking: 'You cast your dreary eyes about, up Baker Street, and it gets worse'.

The reasons for this are not entirely clear. The market, which had been active as late as 1798, was defunct. *Pigot's Directory* of 1826 states that 'the loss of the market has been of considerable injury to the town'. Lamb, writing to Mary Shelley in January 1830, describes the redundant Market Place: 'Clowns stand about what was the Market-place, and spit minutely to relieve ennui'. Also, the enclosure of Enfield Chase had not been the great bonanza that had been expected. The land, mostly stiff clay, had proved intractable and the new farms,

hedged and ditched at great expense, provided little profit for the farmers. There had as yet been little in the way of industrialisation – the Royal Small Arms Factory at Enfield Lock and Grout and Baylis' crape factory at Ponders End were the only establishments of any size.

Enfield then was certainly green and, in parts, pleasant, but it would be a great mistake to regard it as a rural paradise. In fact, large parts of the parish could better be designated a rural slum. A report to the General Board of Health on sanitary conditions in Enfield (1850) reveals a picture of dirt and disease. For drainage Enfield was entirely dependent upon cesspits, open ditches and water-courses. The water supply was largely drawn from shallow wells and was of dubious quality. Many of the places and nuisances cited in the report were located in Enfield Town, Gentleman's Row and Chase Side areas and must have been known to Lamb by sight and probably by smell.

Of the state of health of Enfield in Lamb's time there is little reliable data. A Vestry meeting held on 6 January 1825 noted that a large increase in disease among 'the labouring poor' had resulted in an increased charge on the poor rate. In a letter dated June 1827 Lamb refers to an outbreak of rabies: 'All the dogs are going mad here if you believe the overseers'. Writing to William Hazlitt on 13 September 1831, Lamb refers to Mrs Westwood's daughter being in a fever and her granddaughter having the measles. A much more telling piece of evidence is a paper written by Lamb's friend, Dr Jacob Vale Asbury of Silver Street, entitled 'A Treatise On Epidemic Cholera', published in 1833. Asbury had dealt with at least fifteen cases of this disease in Enfield. His treatment included the use of saline solution and opium and also of mercury ointment and calomel, a chloride of mercury used as a purgative. One must presume that at least some of the patients had survived the treatment, or else the good doctor would not have gone to the trouble of publicising it.

HORSEBUSES

Enfield did not enter the railway era until 1840 and in the meantime passenger traffic remained in the hands of the coach proprietors. The only coach service to and from Enfield Town was provided by John Glover whose vehicles ran from the King's Head in the Market Place to the Flower Pot, Bishopsgate and to the Bell in Holborn, for a fare of 2/6d return. Glover, born in *c*.1803, was a native of Hackney and was later joined in the business by his younger brother, William, who became landlord of the King's Head. A third brother, Newman Glover, lived at Uvedale Cottage in Holly

45. The Market Square in the late 19th century. Apart from the addition of the gas lamp, little had changed since Lamb's day. The market cross was built in 1826 and would have been virtually new when Lamb first came to Enfield.

Walk. Lamb certainly travelled on Glover's coach. A letter to Fanny Kelly dated 25 September 1827 was written 'on the coach from the Bell, Holborn half past three or half past four to the door'. However, Lamb more frequently walked to Edmonton which, being on the main road to Cambridge had a coach every half hour to London. In October 1830 he wrote to Thomas Noon Talfourd: 'The Edmonton stages come almost every hour from Snow Hill'.

FOR THE SONS OF GENTLEFOLK

Enfield at this time had a large number of private boarding schools and Lamb was on friendly terms with the proprietors of at least two of these. He was certainly acquainted with the staff of the Palace School in Enfield Town. This was run by one Thomas May with the assistance of his wife Mary, three teachers and four servants. There were 31 pupils in residence at the time of the 1841 census. Lamb wrote to Mrs May on 3 July 1828 offering thanks for a pleasant evening spent in the company of her and Mr May. A Mr. Sugden who taught for twelve years at this school married the daughter of Mr Westwood in whose house in Chase Side Lamb lodged. In June 1828 Lamb wrote a testimonial for Sugden who was applying for a job at a school run by a Mrs Morgan.

Lamb was also acquainted with a Mrs Mary Gisborne who ran a ladies' boarding school in Baker Street, and he wrote a verse to a Miss Gray/ Grey, a pupil at the school. Charles and Mary Cowden Clarke recalled that, during a visit to the Lambs at Enfield, they were taken to play whist at a schoolmistress's house. On introducing Mary Cowden Clarke to their hostess, Lamb, who was in a mischievous mood, said 'She hopes you have sprats for supper this evening'. As these were then a delicacy of the lower orders, the schoolmistress was not amused.

THE DEMON DRINK

Lamb seems to have been well acquainted with the pubs of Enfield. In a letter to William Hone on 20 June 1827, he writes, 'Can you slip down here and go a Green-dragoning?', no doubt a reference to the Green Dragon in Green Lanes, Winchmore Hill. In *Pigot's Directory* of 1826 the landlord's name was William Boards.

In a letter to Talfourd, 31 January 1828, after outlining the route to Enfield via Essex Road, Newington Green and Green Lanes, he writes 'We are known at the Horseshoes and the Rising Sun'. The Horseshoes, now known as the Crown and Horseshoes, stands on the bank of the New River, close to Chase Side. In 1826 the landlord was one Robert Worrall. It was here on the evening of 19 December 1832 that Lamb, having gone to fetch a pint of porter for Edward Moxon who was a guest

46. The Manor House in use as the Palace School, run by Lamb's friend, Thomas May.

47. *The Crown and Horseshoes, one of Lamb's favourite pubs.*

of the Lambs, fell in with a group of four men playing dominoes. One of them, a young merchant seaman named Benjamin Danby, recognised Lamb as a former customer of his father's hairdresser's shop at the Temple. (In *Pigot's Directory* of 1826 a Henry Danby, perfumer and haircutter, is listed at no.117, Drury Lane.) The next day young Danby's body with its throat cut, was found in a ditch on Holtwhites Hill. Lamb found himself summoned before the Rev. Dr. Daniel Cresswell, Vicar and Chairman of the bench to be questioned about his recollections of the evening. The event gave rise to a lurid broadsheet verse:-

"Give ear ye tender Christians all and listen unto me
While I relate a deed of blood and great barbarity,
A murder of the blackest dye I now repeat in rhyme,
Committed on Benjamin Danby, a young man in his prime.

This young man was a sailor, and just returned from sea,
And down to Enfield Chase he went his cousin for to see,
With money in his pocket so jolly and so free,
But little did he dream of such dismal destiny.

Twas on a Wednesday evening he called at the Horse Shoe,
And there drank so freely, as mostly sailors do,
So ruffians in the company whom he did treat most kind,
To rob and murder him that night most wickedly designed.

They threw him on the ground and stabbed him with a knife,
He cried out 'Don't murder me! - O do not take my life!'
But heedless of his piteous cries, his throat they cut so deep.
And turned the gully in his throat as butchers kill their sheep.

Then in a ditch they threw his corpse, mangled with ghastly
    wounds,
Where early the next morning the body it was found.
Now Cooper, Fare and Johnson are committed for this crime,
And will be tried at Newgate all in a little time".

The Rising Sun stood on the south side of Church Street more or less opposite the junction with Little Park Gardens. It survived until 1933, when it was demolished for road widening, the licence and the name being transferred to a new pub in Edmonton at the junction of Chichester Road and Bury Street.

Another public house known to Lamb was the Rose and Crown in Clay Hill. Charles and Mary Cowden Clarke describe a long walk in the company of the Lambs and Fanny Kelly. The company stopped to refresh themselves at a wayside inn. The description – heavily wooded surroundings, the dip in the road, the ford and the footbridge – tallies perfectly with the Rose and Crown. Today, apart from the substitution of a bridge for the ford, the scene has scarcely altered.

RICKBURNING

A letter Lamb wrote to George Dyer on 20 December 1830 provides evidence of Enfield's involvement in the agricultural workers' uprising of 1830/31, which took the form of a wave of rickburning across southern and eastern England. Lamb describes the firing of seven haystacks belonging to a farmer whom Lamb calls Graystock, but whose real name was Daniel Poyser. The night before he saw flames in the sky about half a mile away. Middlesex experienced little of this campaign of arson, the counties worst affected being Kent, Berkshire and Hampshire, and there were several major outbreaks in Essex. However, a few days previously on 15 December, there had been an incident at Wrotham Park, Potters Bar on the far side of Enfield Chase. An analysis of the reported incidents shows that they began in north-east Essex close to the Cambridgeshire border and moved southwards before finally spilling over the border into Middlesex. (See *Captain Swing* by Eric Hobsbawm and George Rudé (1969).

Lamb appears to have had little sympathy for the desperate plight of the agricultural labourers that drove them to rickburning: 'It was never good times in England since the poor began to speculate upon their condition. Formerly they jogged along with as little reflection as horses: the whistling ploughman went cheek by jowl with his brother that neighed. Now the biped carries a box of phosphorous in his leather breeches, and in the dead of night the half illuminated beast steals his magic potion into a cleft in a barn, and half a country is grinning with new fires'. He was clearly of the opinion that the ricks had been fired by a disaffected labourer. 'Farmer Graystock says something to the touchy rustic that he did not relish, and he writes his distaste in flames'.

48. The Rose and Crown, Clay Hill, looking much the same as when Lamb visited it.

FRIENDS AND NEIGHBOURS

Of the people with whom Lamb came into contact in Enfield three are of importance: Jacob Vale Asbury, Dr Daniel Cresswell, the Vicar and John Tuff, a pharmacist.

Tuff figures only once in Lamb's letters – Lamb wrote to him from Edmonton in 1833 concerning tickets for a performance at Covent Garden. He was born *c*.1801 in the village of Stilton, Huntingdonshire, and so would have been in his early thirties when Lamb knew him. By 1826, he was a pharmacist with a shop in Enfield Town next to the George, and was married with two daughters, both of whom became schoolteachers. His chief claim to local fame is his book *Historical Notices of Enfield* published in 1859. It is badly written and arranged, but is nevertheless one of the most useful sources on nineteenth-century Enfield. It contains brief biographical notes on Lamb in such an impersonal tone that no one would guess that Tuff had actually known the famous author.

Daniel Cresswell, the Vicar, is one of Lamb's few Enfield acquaintances whom he specifically describes as a friend. He was appointed to Enfield in 1823 and remained there until his death at the age of 68 in the spring of 1844. He was an accomplished classical scholar and a mathematician of some repute, the author of a number of books on

mathematics. He took an active interest in parish affairs, taking the chair at Vestry meetings, and among the achievements of his incumbency were the rebuilding of the south aisle of the church in 1826, improvements at the workhouse and the establishment of the National School in Enfield

49. John Tuff's chemist's shop on the right, near The George c.1870. Lamb was one of his customers.

50. *John Tuff c.1870.*

Town in 1839. During his time three chapels of ease were also constructed (*see p74*). He was a rather old-fashioned evangelical and in his last years was to have trouble from High Church supporters in the parish.

Apart from Cresswell, Jacob Vale Asbury was Lamb's principal friend in Enfield. His name is mentioned several times in Lamb's letters. In December 1828, writing to Louisa Holcroft whose family was afflicted with measles, Lamb feigned a fear of catching the disease: 'I will send for Mr. Asbury'. In April 1830, when Lamb's ward, Emma Isola, was ill at Enfield some bottles of medicine prescribed by Asbury were delivered. These were labelled 'Miss Isola Lamb', a mistake that amused Lamb. Writing to Edward Moxon in March 1833 Lamb reported that he had burnt his leg and was being attended by Asbury. That Lamb mixed socially with Asbury is clear from another letter in which he apologises for having drunk too much at Asbury's house and recalls being carried home along Parsonage Lane to Chase Side.

Asbury was born *c.*1792, a native of Stafford-

shire. There is no precise information of when he came to Enfield, but on 4 May 1820 he was married in St Andrew's Church to Dorothy Jacomb, whose family had owned property in Enfield since 1791. Mrs Asbury was two years older than her husband and was born in Basinghall Street in the City of London. The Asburys, who had three sons and two daughters, lived at White Lodge, a large clapboard house still standing in Silver Street. At the time of the 1851 census he employed two medical assistants, a coachman, a cook and two housemaids. In 1837 he bought a coach house adjoining his premises for the sum of £50.

Asbury was parish surgeon for Enfield, though it is not clear when he was appointed, but in 1837 he became medical officer to Enfield Workhouse, then used for housing the parish children. Asbury carried out his duties conscientiously and was particularly concerned with attempts to eradicate skin diseases such as ringworm and scabies, which were endemic among the children.

He was also involved in efforts to solve public health problems in Enfield. Much of the data contained in the General Board of Health Report for Enfield was supplied by him and this led to the setting up of the Enfield Local Board of Health in 1850. He died in June 1871 and was buried in St Andrew's churchyard. His daughter, Mary Susannah Asbury, lived on in Enfield until her death in April 1908 at the age of 82, but sadly whatever she knew about her father and his most famous patient she kept to herself.

The activities of Lamb and his associates provide an interesting insight into Enfield life in the early nineteenth century. Great changes were afoot and Enfield was soon to be subjected to a process of suburbanisation that was to result in it being totally engulfed by London.

51. *White Lodge, Silver Street, home of Lamb's physician, Dr. Jacob Vale Asbury.*

A Rising Suburb
Enfield 1850-1870

THE RAILWAY ERA

By 1850 Enfield had entered the railway era. In 1840 the Northern & Eastern Railway opened the first section of its main line between Stratford and Broxbourne. The company had ambitions to build a trunk line from London to York via Cambridge, but its finances were not equal to the task. The line had barely passed Bishops Stortford when the supply of money gave out and the company was taken over by the Eastern Counties Railway, whose Shoreditch terminus it had been sharing since 1840. (In 1862 the ECR was to merge with other companies in East Anglia to form the Great Eastern Railway, a much more potent concern.)

The Lea Valley Line was built along the floor of the valley to save engineering costs with the unintended result that most of the stations were poorly sited, well away from the main areas of settlement. Enfield was served by Ponders End Station, located at the eastern end of South Street, close to the Lee Navigation. In 1845 Ponders End was served by five trains each way daily, while in Edmonton, Water Lane (Angel Road) – a bad location, had just three.

An extra station opened at Ordnance Road in 1855 to serve the Royal Small Arms factory. Originally called Ordnance Factory, it was later renamed Enfield Lock. At first it had staggered platforms, either side of a level crossing – this primitive arrangement can still be seen at Roydon, between Broxbourne and Harlow. Enfield Lock station was later rebuilt on more conventional lines.

In 1846 an Act authorised a branch line to Enfield Town promoted by a locally floated subsidiary of the ECR called the Edmonton & Enfield Railway

52. John Clarke's former school building in use as a railway station shortly before demolition in 1872.

53. The former level crossing at Bury Street, now replaced by a bridge.

Company, the directors of which were all Enfield men. One was William Hainworth, proprietor of a boys' boarding school in Nags Head Lane (Southbury Road), an establishment previously owned by John Clarke, during whose time John Keats had been a pupil (*see p131*). Hainworth, exhibiting a finer grasp of finance than business ethics, managed to sell the school building to the company for use as the terminus, and then promptly vanished from Enfield. Another factor, which may have expedited the building of the line was the involvement of David Waddington, Vice Chairman and later Chairman of the ECR. From 1847 to 1857 he was living at Adelaide House, Forty Hill (*see p72*).

Leaving the Lea Valley Line at Water Lane the single track branch ran north-west to the new terminus at Enfield Town (built behind the old school house), with one intermediate station at Edmonton Green. The site of this low-level station is now covered by Edmonton Green roundabout.

The new line opened in 1849 mainly served by a shuttle between Enfield and Water Lane, supplemented by through trains to Shoreditch in the morning and evening peak periods. The fares were

54. Ponders End Station still standing more or less in its original state in 1955.

55. Houses in Napier Road, Ponders End, 1955.

relatively expensive, the trains ran by a circuitous route via Stratford, and the Shoreditch terminus was not very conveniently sited. Nonetheless, it soon killed off Glover's omnibus service, which had ceased running by 1855.

The Great Northern Railway opened the first section of its main line between London and Peterborough in 1850. This crossed the extreme western edge of Enfield at Hadley Wood, where some very heavy tunnelling work had to be carried out. The nearest stations to Enfield were initially Barnet and Potters Bar, no station being provided at Hadley Wood until many years later.

THE BUILDERS MOVE IN

From 1851, census figures show Enfield's population growing until at last, hemmed in to the north by Green Belt restrictions and approaching saturation point elsewhere, a ceiling was reached in 1951. In 1851 it stood at 9,453, just 86 more than ten years previously but by 1861 it was 12,424 and in 1871, 16,054.

In Enfield Town, building in Cecil Road, Raleigh Road, Essex Road and Sydney Road began in 1853. The main frontages along Essex Road and London Road were developed with large middle-class houses, while tucked out of sight in Raleigh Road and Sydney Road, the houses were much smaller, intended for the artisan class.

In 1854 the Conservative Land Society began to develop Burleigh Road, Queens Road, Stanley Road and an adjoining stretch fronting Southbury Road. This scheme was unsuccessful and there were still vacant plots on these streets into the twentieth century. Some houses built in Southbury Road remained untenanted for so many years that they were nicknamed 'Gibraltar Villas' because they were so long untaken.

North of Enfield Town, Gordon Road was laid out on the site of the demolished Gordon House;

this was commenced in 1858. Then the pace of development slackened and in nearby Halifax Road serious building did not start until the 1870s. In the north-west angle between Lancaster Road and Baker Street, Canton Road had been built by 1861. This was a poor road and in the early days blocked drains were a frequent problem. (This road now forms part of Primrose Avenue.)

At Forty Hill the Bridgenhall Estate was sold in 1868. The roads laid out at this time include Russell Road, St George's Road and Avenue Road (Garnault Road), but there is not much evidence of serious building on this estate prior to the 1880s.

At Ponders End, Alma Road was built by 1855 and by 1867 Napier Road and New Road were under construction. At Enfield Wash, Jasper Road was built by 1867 and in 1871 there were houses in Bell Lane. South of Ordnance Road, Alma Road and Grove Road were built in the late 1850s and at the eastern end, close to the Royal Small Arms factory, Warwick Road and Medcalf Road were occupied by 1861. The Putney Lodge Estate was sold in 1867 and four years later Putney Road, Totteridge Road and Mandeville Road had been built. The last three developments were primarily for workers at the Royal Small Arms factory.

BUSINESS LIFE

Details of the commercial life of Enfield can be pieced together using directories, especially the Kelly's Directories of 1845 and 1855, and more information can be distilled from the 1851 census.

John Prior Patman was the biggest builder in Enfield. He was born c.1777 at Granchester near Cambridge and had been in Enfield since the mid 1820s, when he took over the business of his uncle, Lawrence Patman. Additionally, he was the Enfield agent for Royal Exchange Insurance. At the time of the 1851 census he employed 25 men. By 1855 he had died and the business was being run by his widow, Ann. The firm did a fair amount of contract work for the newly-formed Enfield Local Board of Health, including some sewer pipework in Chase Side, which turned out to be defective and had to be relaid. On the other hand, two bridges constructed by the firm – at Clay Hill and Slades Hill – both lasted more than 140 years.

Thomas Cutbush, born in Whitechapel c.1809, ran a much smaller business than Patman, with just two men working for him in 1851. He was a plumber and paperhanger, operating from premises at the junction of London Road and The Town, for which he paid his landlord, Ebenezer Gibbons, an annual rent of £30. Like Patman, he regularly did contract work for the Local Board, including painting all the lampposts.

Henry Rising was a silk mercer and linen draper

56. *William Lock's drapery shop (right) formerly owned by Henry Rising and later taken over by the Pearson Brothers. To the left can be seen the office of the Enfield Observer (founded in 1859), the direct ancestor of the Enfield Gazette.*

with a shop at the corner of Church Street and Slaughterhouse Lane (Sydney Road). He was born *c*.1813 at Lyng, near East Dereham, and had been in Enfield Town since at least 1839. His name appears regularly in the accounts of the Enfield British School in Chase Side as supplying sewing materials for use in needlework lessons. By 1855 the business had been sold on to William Easter, who later sold it to William Lock. In 1902 it was bought by the Pearson Brothers, whose department store is still in business in Enfield Town.

Thomas Parbery was a blacksmith and ironmonger with premises on Chase Green which are currently occupied by Newsons. He was born at Weybridge, Surrey, and was established in Enfield by 1839. In 1851 Parbery employed two men. He died at the age of 87 in 1895 and was buried in St Andrew's Churchyard where the gravestone can still be seen. The forge was later taken over by the Wiggett family.

Thomas Brading's grocery was in Ponders End High Street. He was born at Bethnal Green *c*.1810 and seems to have settled in Ponders End during the late 1830s. In 1845 the shop was also home to the Ponders End Post Office, but by 1855 this had moved to a tailor's shop run by Henry Guiver. In 1859 Brading became secretary to the Ponders End Gas Company and in 1871, by now retired, he was still living in the area. A nonconformist, he was a member of the Ponders End Congregational

Church, and in the autumn of 1853 he organised a 'no popery' mob which disrupted a poll of the vestry voters to settle the dispute over new pews for St Andrew's Church (*see p72*).

CONVIVIAL ENFIELD

The 1855 *Kelly's Directory* lists 63 pubs in Enfield. (The directory has separate entries for Enfield and Ponders End, which, for the purposes of this book, have been treated as one.) Most of them were proper public houses with a full licence and a name, but others were mere beershops, licensed for beer and wine only. The latter were not normally mentioned by name in directories, but in many cases their identities can be established from other sources. Some survive to this day as conventional public houses.

In Enfield Town, The Greyhound stood on the corner of The Town and the Market Square, a large brick building with Dutch gables, clearly of early seventeenth century date. The landlord in 1855 was Robert Edward Docking, probably related to John Docking, who ran the King's Head at Edmonton Green. The Greyhound was soon to lose its licence, and was used after 1860 as public offices and a court house. The building was demolished in 1897 to make way for the Enfield Town branch of the London and Provincial Bank, now Barclays. (The author's grandfather, then aged seven,

57. The former Greyhound Inn c.1868. The site is now occupied by the Enfield Town branch of Barclay's Bank.

watched the bank being built.)

At the rear of the Market Square stood the King's Head, still run by William Glover, although his family's horse bus business had been killed by railway competition. Photographs show a prim Georgian building, but other records tell a different story, the smells emanating from the urinal being a regular source of public complaint. The pub was rebuilt in 1899 and still retains some superb engraved glass from this period.

On the north side of The Town stood the Railway Inn, formerly The Rummer, run by Edwin Mabbet. Much rebuilt and much renamed, it survives today as The Coach House. Facing it across the road is The George, run in 1855 by Robert Mathison. It was then a large early Georgian brick building with a long frontage and a yard and stabling behind; it was rebuilt in 1895.

The Nag's Head, which gave its name to Nags Head Lane (now Southbury Road), was in the hands of George Rixon. Rebuilt at least twice, it eventually closed *c.*1960, and the building is currently used for a Pizza Hut. (For The Rising Sun in Church Street *see p44*). On the fringes of The Town, Charles Pettey ran a beershop called The White Horse in Silver Street, and, beside the then new railway terminus, the Enfield Arms had been built.

North of The Town, in Baker Street stood The Bell and The Wheatsheaf, plus four beershops. At opposite ends of Chase Side stood The Crown and Horseshoes and The Holly Bush, and another four. In Parsonage Lane stood The Old Sergeant, now the only building of any age to survive in that road. There was also a small beershop in Brigadier Hill run by Thomas Sanders. His wife, Sally Sanders, worked as a pig breeder and dealer, a business which proved to be a major public health problem.

At Forty Hill the only pub was The Goat, then standing at the corner of Goat Lane and Forty Hill.

58. The King's Head, newly rebuilt in 1899.

59. *The George c.1870. The pub was rebuilt in 1895.*

60. *The Goat, Forty Hill, c.1905. The building is now a private house.*

(The present pub at Forty Hill Green was built in the late 1920s, the former building, much altered, surviving as a private house.) Nearby, Bulls Cross was served by The Pied Bull and a beershop. The latter, known as The Spotted Cow, lost its licence after World War I, but the building remains as a private house called The Orchards. At Clay Hill, The Fallow Buck and The Rose and Crown, both houses of some antiquity, competed for trade with a beershop. In Whitewebbs Lane there was William Harrison's beershop.

On The Chase there were three pubs and three beershops. The Cock stood by the gate to Hadley Common at Cockfosters and The Chequers stood at Coopers Lane, run by Benjamin Williams, who also worked as a farrier. (This pub was transferred to Potters Bar in 1924 as a result of boundary adjustment.) The Ridge Road Inn stood on the west side of The Ridgeway, slightly to the south of its modern replacement, The Ridgeway Tavern. On Windmill Hill stood two beershops, one of them run by William Collins. He also worked as a rat

61. *The Pied Bull at Bulls Cross c.1890.*

62. *The Fallow Buck at Clay Hill c.1890.*

63. *The Swan and Pike near the Royal Small Arms Factory. It closed during World War I and never reopened.*

catcher, possibly one of a number of ratcatchers in Enfield who supplied live rats to sporting pubs in London for rat-killing matches. On Enfield Chase (location unspecified) was a beershop run by James Ward, who also worked as a farmer.

In Ponders End there were six pubs and three beershops. Along the High Street stood The White Hart, The Two Brewers, and The Goat, plus a beershop, now The Boundary House. The Pike and Anchor stood close to the River Lee and in South Street were to be found The Falcon and The Railway Tavern.

Enfield Highway and Enfield Wash were generously provided. Along the Hertford Road lay The Plough, The Rose and Crown, The King's Arms, The Red Lion, The Black Horse, The White Lion and The Sun & Woolpack. Elsewhere in East Enfield there were two beershops in Green Street, probably the direct ancestors of The Golden Hive and The White Horse. In Turkey Street there were two beershops, plus one in Hoe Lane and another in Carterhatch Lane. At Enfield Lock The Swan and Pike stood alongside the River Lee, and The Canteen, later the Ordnance Arms, served workers at the Royal Small Arms factory.

THE NEW POOR LAW

Under the Poor Law Amendment Act of 1834 Enfield was incorporated into the Edmonton Poor Law Union which also included Hornsey, Tottenham, Edmonton, Waltham Abbey and Cheshunt. In 1837 the poor relief responsibilities of these parishes were taken over by this new authority whose first act was to build a new workhouse in Silver Street, Edmonton – parts of that building survive incorporated in the North Middlesex Hospital. On completion in 1842, most of the former parish workhouses were closed. The Enfield Workhouse (there had been one on its site since 1719) was fairly new,

64. *St Michael's Hospital, Chase Side, incorporating much of the former Enfield Workhouse of 1826.*

65. The Chase Farm School, built in 1886.

having been rebuilt in 1827, and this was adapted to house pauper children from all the parishes within the Union. It was used for this until the construction of a purpose-built orphanage (Chase Farm School) in 1886 and was then used to house the elderly infirm.

In 1930 the Edmonton Union was superseded by Middlesex County Council. Chase Farm School became a general hospital in 1939 and then part of the National Health Service in 1948 as did the geriatric hospital in the former workhouse – it was renamed St Michael's Hospital. The building was demolished in 1997 and the site redeveloped for housing.

THE LONG ARM OF THE LAW

The parish constables of Enfield were made redundant in 1840 when the district became part of the N Division of the Metropolitan Police and the Vestry House in Enfield Town became a police station. The first station sergeant, John Coote, aged 35, was listed in the 1841 census as living over the police station with his wife and two children. This building sufficed for some years, but was replaced in 1872 by a larger police station at the junction of London Road and Cecil Road. (This was replaced by the present police station in Silver Street in 1965.)

A police station was built at Green Street in 1849, superseded by more sumptuous premises in the Hertford Road. (The present Ponders End Police Station, serving the whole of East Enfield, opened in 1970.)

66. The Enfield Town Police Station in London Road in 1909.

THE LOCAL BOARD TAKES OVER

Prior to 1850 Enfield was governed by a select vestry, one established by Act of Parliament and which itself filled any vacancies which occurred. This body conducted itself in a distinctly leisurely fashion. Reading through its minutes for the period 1830-50 it becomes clear that its principal concerns were the parish church and the parish charities. Responsibility for Poor Law had passed to the Edmonton Board of Guardians in 1837, and one looks in vain for evidence of social conditions or public health problems. Nothing would suggest that the parish was other than prosperous, well governed and healthy. However, this impression is distinctly misleading, since other sources reveal a very different picture

The 1848 Public Health Act signalled the determination of central government to tackle local public health problems. A new government department, the General Board of Health under the direction of the formidable Edwin Chadwick was established, beneath which were Local Boards of Health established on petition by ratepayers and elected on a ratepayer franchise. The powers of these Boards were more wide ranging than the their title suggests and included sewerage, drainage, water supply, street management, the making and maintenance of burial grounds and the regulation of offensive trades.

THE RURAL SLUM

In the spring of 1849, as a result of a petition probably compiled by some Enfield residents, William Ranger, Superintending Inspector to the General Board of Health arrived to make investigations. The Enfield Vestry was clearly upset by this and refused to form a committee to meet him. This attitude was in marked contrast to that of Edmonton Vestry which co-operated with the General Board of Health's investigation later the same year.

Ranger's report paints a lurid picture of living conditions in Enfield. The water supply was drawn from the New River, from wells or from rainwater cisterns in the roofs of houses. The wells were mostly contaminated. Many poor people could only obtain water from public houses, for which privilege they were forced to purchase beer.

Sanitation was primitive. In Loves Row (now Chapel Street) there was a ditch four feet wide to carry away sewage, completely choked with rubbish. Parsonage Lane was served by an open sewer. The Holly Bush end of Chase Side was utterly disease ridden and there were many pools of stagnant water. Anderson's Cottages in Baker Street were drained by an open ditch, choked with offal from a local butcher. Even parts of the Town had open ditches and cesspits. Slaughterhouse Lane (Sydney Road) and the cottages in the Market

67. Meeting House Yard (Baker Street), a public health trouble spot of long standing.

Place were particularly offensive. At Gloucester Place in Chase Side there was only one gully hole for the entire row and this was near the water pump. At Meeting House Yard in Baker Street slops were simply thrown out of the doors back and front. At South Place, Ponders End, were 22 houses containing 115 people; here the sewage was carried away by an open ditch only eight feet from the back doors.

The custom of keeping animals on the premises was widespread. In Meeting House Yard people kept pigs in their cottages and some dwellings in Brigadier Hill were in an offensive state from pigs' manure and decomposed vegetable matter.

Three people are mentioned by Ranger as having been of special assistance to him. These were Rev. John Moore Heath, the much-maligned Vicar of Enfield (*see p72*), Dr Asbury and Dr John Millar, a Scottish doctor practising in Baker Street. For want of other evidence, these three must be regarded as the prime movers in involving the General Board of Health in Enfield's affairs. Ranger's report ends with the recommendation that a Local Board of Health be set up in Enfield.

LOCAL DEMOCRACY

The election of the first Enfield Local Board of Health took place on 3 August 1850. Members were elected by the entire parish, as there was no system of warding as in modern local government elections. The degree of interest aroused can be judged by the fact that 28 candidates competed for the twelve seats on the board. The successful ones included a mixture of gentry and tradesmen. Four gave their occupation as 'gentleman' and the Vicar can be added to their numbers. There was one doctor, three farmers, a wheelwright and a builder. The result was fairly representative of Enfield's population. Geographically the lack of a ward system produced strange results with just two members from East Enfield, the Board thus being dominated by members from Enfield Town. All the successful candidates had experience on the Vestry and one was a former Churchwarden.

The first meeting of the Board took place on 19 August 1850 at which James Meyer of Forty Hall was unanimously elected chairman. He was to hold this office without a break until his death in 1894, shortly before the Local Board gave way to the Urban District Council. John Sawyer, an Enfield Town solicitor, was appointed Clerk, Henry Young Surveyor and Inspector of Nuisances. Mordaunt Martin Monro, an elected member, was appointed Treasurer but in 1854 a firm of bankers, Messrs. Dimsdale Drewett and Fowler were appointed as treasurers to the Board.

68. James Meyer of Forty Hall, chairman of the Enfield Local Board of Health 1850-94.

STAFF PROBLEMS

John Sawyer was a distinctly shady character, and held a large number of offices. He was Clerk to the Edmonton Union and Superintendent Registrar of Birth, Marriages and Deaths. He was Steward of the Manors of Enfield, Worcesters and the Rectory. His employment by the Edmonton Union occasionally caused problems for when the Union and the Board were in dispute, Sawyer was in the Gilbertian situation of writing letters to himself, but the conflict of interest did not appear to trouble him unduly. He was also Clerk to Enfield Vestry. His responsibilities included maintaining a register of plans, keeping accounts and checking orders and vouchers. In 1851 his salary was fixed at £30 p.a. Sadly, Sawyer was given to the vice of nepotism. His brother, William Clayton Sawyer, became a rate collector, but resigned from this post for unspecified reasons in September 1856, it later emerging that W.C. Sawyer had embezzled £154 of the Board's money, the sum being repaid by his brother.

In 1859 another brother, Arthur Sawyer, was given the task of making a preliminary survey for a sewer. In January 1857 John Sawyer's salary was increased to £150 p.a. on condition that he provided a competent person to assist him on Local Board business, but this condition does not appear to have been complied with. In December 1858 Sawyer was reported to be in failing health and it was suggested he share his duties with his partner Francis Walker. This was done, but does not seem to have been satisfactory, for in September 1859 Walker resigned. By December 1859 Sawyer's health had declined to such an extent that he was no longer capable of carrying out his duties and he resigned, dying on 7 January 1860.

Sawyer's successor was Edward Letchworth who was to hold the office of Clerk for most of the remainder of the Local Board's existence. He was a brisk and efficient man and there is no suspicion that he was corrupt. In his old age he was to achieve a knighthood for his services to freemasonry and he became Grand Secretary of the English Freemasons in 1892. He died in 1917 at the age of 84.

Henry Young, the Surveyor and Inspector of Nuisances, in contrast to Sawyer seems to have been of unimpeachable honesty, but the conduct of his duties was somewhat idiosyncratic. At the time of his appointment to the Board he was distinctly elderly if not old, having previously served the Vestry as Road Surveyor. In April 1853 the work of Inspector of Nuisances was taken away from him and given to Richard Watkin, and in December 1855 William Ironside, a former elected member of the Board, was given the post of Surveyor. Young continued as Highway Surveyor. This separation of posts seems to be indicative of Young's advancing years and his inability to carry out all the duties he had taken on. Late in December 1855, the Board received a heavily sarcastic letter from a John Goswell of South Street complaining of poor road maintenance in Ponders End. According to him, 'a very old infirm man is seen at very long intervals affecting to scrape here and there'. The old man referred to is almost certainly Henry Young. It is also clear that Young frequently acted in total disregard of the orders of the Board, for in April 1856 he was told not to undertake work without prior authorisation. Keeping proper records of expenditure does not appear to have been one of his strong points. After repeated warnings, he was told in August 1858 that his salary would be withheld unless he produced proper accounts. In December 1858 the Board decided that Young was too old for his work, but would not dismiss him in view of his past services. His salary at that time was £100 p.a. In August

1861 Stephen Lancaster Lucena complained that Young, in the course of his work, had caused damage to his fence on Windmill Hill. The Board was by now clearly tired of covering up for Young's erratic behaviour and replied that the damage was done without its authority and that Lucena would have to seek redress from Young personally. Young continued until December 1866 when he wrote a dignified if ungrammatical letter of resignation on the grounds of old age and ill health. He had served the Vestry and Local Board for a total of 45 years.

Ironside, appointed surveyor in 1855, seems to have been competent if uninspired. His surviving report books show that he was semi-literate – his spelling was poor and he used no punctuation whatever.

BUILDING CONTROL

The Board made an immediate impact in building control. No new building was allowed unless plans had been approved. The purpose of this was to ensure that houses were built with adequate drains and water supply. In November 1850 a Mr Lovegrove of West Ham submitted plans for some cottages in Green Street, which were rejected because they showed no provision for drainage. This did not deter him and he re-submitted them with minor amendments. These were again rejected because they showed no levels and no sanitation. In March 1852 the Board took out a summons against a builder who had begun erecting cottages in Brigadier Hill without permission. It is clear that many builders at this time used only the skimpiest of plans if they bothered using any at all. Vigilance and determined action by the Board brought the recalcitrant builders to heel very quickly.

HEALTH PROBLEMS

In the field of public health the Board's achievements were less spectacular. Under the terms of the 1848 Act they were obliged to appoint a Surveyor and an Inspector of Nuisances. This was done, as we have seen with the appointment of the aged Mr Young, in a distinctly cheeseparing manner with both combined. The appointment of a Medical Officer of Health, however, was optional and the Board did not choose to exercise this expensive option.

In February 1851 the Board purchased lime chloride for distribution to those too poor to afford it. Lime chloride was then the principal disinfecting agent in use, but there is no record that any of it was ever distributed. In September 1853 the

General Board of Health warned of a renewed outbreak of cholera. At the same time a letter was received from George Rumsey of Gordon House, Chase Side, complaining about an offensive ditch behind the Workhouse and warning of the danger of cholera, but no action was taken. In August 1854 an outbreak of cholera occurred in Brigadier Hill, starting at the home of a family by the name of Hockett. In March 1854 Rev. Robert Tabor, Vicar of Christ Church, Cockfosters, wrote complaining about the insanitary state of Mill Corner, Hadley. Again, no action was taken and Tabor later wrote a letter to the General Board which described in harrowing detail an outbreak of cholera at precisely the spot about which he had warned the Enfield Board six months previously. A major outbreak of cholera had occurred in Soho, killing over five hundred people between the 1st and 10th. A family by the name of Slade fled from their home in Regent Street and headed north, hoping to escape the infection. They stayed overnight at an inn at Hadley where the wife, Mary Slade, died from cholera. The disease spread rapidly, resulting in fifty cases and nine deaths. The General Board of Health was particularly anxious to know why Tabor's warning should have been ignored. In 1862 there was an outbreak of smallpox. In April of that year the Clerk to the Edmonton Union wrote to the Board reporting eight cases at Enfield Highway, and later the same month a case at Cockfosters was reported by Archibald Paris of Greenwood Plain, Hadley Wood, a member of the Board. The involvement of a Board member resulted in an unusually vigorous response and a reluctant Mr Ironside was despatched to burn infected bedding and treat the walls of the cottage with chloride of lime.

SEWERAGE

The Board's efforts in the provision of a sewage system was somewhat spasmodic. In February 1851 it was decided to conduct a survey. This was undoubtedly needed, for the parish relied almost entirely upon privies and ditches for sewage disposal. Enfield Town had a hodge-podge of privies and barrel drains, most of the effluent finding its way eventually into Saddlers Mill Stream. At last in 1854 James Pilbrow, a civil engineer resident in Tottenham, drew up plans for water supply and sewerage and the General Board of Health gave Enfield permission to borrow £12,500 for these works. The new sewerage system, if it could be called such, was built in a haphazard manner, with no attempt at co-ordination within the whole parish. The only districts to be sewered in the first phase were Ponders End and Enfield Town. The Ponders End sewer drained into the Lee and in Enfield

Town a pipe was laid along Chase Side and through the Town ending in a tank beside the railway in Lincoln Road. From here the effluent passed through a culvert under the railway and into a ditch from where it found its way into Saddlers Mill Stream. The construction of sewers across private land provided landowners with a heaven-sent opportunity to claim compensation from the Board. Some of the claims were almost certainly fraudulent. Mr Lovekin of Chase Side lodged one for £67 in October 1855 alleging structural damage to his house, but he was eventually bought off with £10. By April 1856 the Enfield Town sewerage system, such as it was, was functional and work was well advanced at Ponders End.

The outfall at Lincoln Road was to be a source of trouble, leading ultimately to a battle with the Edmonton Local Board. In July 1856 a letter was received from George Ellis, a farmer from Bury Street and a member of the Edmonton Board, about the state of Saddlers Mill Stream. He claimed that the water was so foul that his cattle refused to drink it. No action was taken. In June 1857 Ellis wrote again and was told that Enfield Local Board reserved the right to use the stream as an outfall. At the same time Ellis raised the matter at a meeting of the Edmonton Board and later that summer two more letters were received on the same subject, one of the complainants asserting that one of his cows had died as a result of drinking the polluted water. In June 1858 a further letter signed by five Edmonton residents was sent to the Enfield Board, accompanied by a medical certificate signed by Henry Hammond, the leading doctor in Edmonton. The Board formed a committee to examine the nuisance, and decided to build a series of deodorising tanks at the outfall. By now the Edmonton Board had also taken up the matter and was pressing Enfield to action. The tanks were rapidly constructed, but despite the recommendation of Mr Pilbrow that the tanks should be filled with broken brick and gravel as a filtering medium, the Board decided to use coke which was cheaper. when the tanks were used the filtering process proved ineffective and in November the Edmonton Surveyor reported the continued pollution of the stream and even produced a bottle of the effluent for the inspection of Board members. In February 1859 a sample of the water was examined by William Ragg, a pharmacist of Edmonton Green, who found it to be contaminated with organic matter, and the Edmonton Board then moved to take proceedings against Enfield. In March a deputation from Enfield attended a meeting of the Edmonton Board to discuss the matter. The Enfield Board proposed to build a new sewer along Lincoln Road to conduct the effluent to the Ponders End outfall, but in return for this it expected a financial contribution from Edmonton of one third of the cost of £700. Edmonton offered a token £50. In May the Home Office made vain efforts to arbitrate and in August the case came to court where Edmonton was granted an injunction restraining Enfield from discharging effluent into Saddlers Mill Stream as from 27 September. Enfield was then faced with building the Lincoln Road sewer as fast as possible. To make matters worse Tottenham Local Board, worried about pollution of the Lee, then threatened proceedings against Enfield, but luckily this came to nothing. The new works were completed in March 1860, thus ending a sorry tale of cheeseparing and incompetence.

WATER SUPPLY

The waterworks, like the sewerage system, was to have a somewhat chequered career. Plans for a waterworks were drawn up in 1854 by Pilbrow at the same time as his work on the sewerage system. The two went hand in hand, for the use of water closets was dependent upon adequate supplies of water. In August 1854 a plot of land in what was to become Alma Road was purchased for £200 for the pumping station and a reservoir site in Holtwhites Hill was bought for £100 early the following year. The pumping engines were made by Headley and Manning of Cambridge and by April 1856 the system of water supply was in operation. It was shown to a visiting inspector from the General Board of Health, Alfred Dickens, a brother of the novelist Charles Dickens. But by March 1857 there was a serious shortage of water. Pilbrow declared that this was caused by waste on the part of consumers, but this view was not shared by Mr Ironside or the engineman. In exasperation the Board called in another engineer, Nathaniel Beardmore, to examine the installation, who reported that while the demand was 64,000 gallons daily, the pumps were only capable of lifting 42,000

69. *Alma Road waterworks, showing the pumping engines.*

70. *Alma Road waterworks, showing the engine house and chimney.*

gallons and recommended increasing the size of the sump at the pumping station. The intervention of Beardmore upset Pilbrow who promptly resigned as consulting engineer. Meanwhile, as the summer advanced, supplies became more erratic and in July an irate letter was received from Alderman Challis of Baker Street claiming that he had had no water for four days. In November 1858 the engine pistons were in a bad way and were examined by the manufacturers who disclaimed any responsibility, stating that the pistons should have been examined every six months, but had been allowed to run for three years without inspection. In June 1860 Beardmore reported that the reservoir was too small, holding less than a day's supply. The water pressure in Ponders End was excessively high because the supply was drawn directly from the pumping main linked up with the reservoir and thus the smallest of pipe-bursts could rapidly assume major proportions. He advocated a new 9" rising main from the pumping station to the reservoir, retaining the old main to serve Ponders End. He also proposed a second reservoir and an additional well in Nags Head Lane. No action was taken and meanwhile complaints about the supply continued. In March 1864 the engine house chimney was reported to be leaning, and there was a two-week break in water supply while a replacement was built. In June 1865 a decision was made to build the low service reservoir in Nags Head Lane, which at least promised a much-needed increase in capacity.

OFFENSIVE TRADES

Enfield Local Board was also responsible for the control of offensive trades. In July 1851 notice was served on all slaughterhouse owners requiring them to register with the Board. In September 1851 a complaint was received concerning one Thomas Brown, a furniture dealer of Enfield Town, for obstructing the pavement with his wares. He was summonsed, convicted and duly fined for this offence. In February 1852 Edward Topping of Fuller House, South Street, complained about the activities of his neighbour Mr Gibbons. The latter made a living by collecting dung and rotten vegetables, which he sold as manure. Mr Topping objected to the smell, which he claimed made his wife and children ill. The matter was referred to the General Board of Health who told Enfield to take court action. In May 1863 a complaint was received concerning the offensive state of the premises of Mr Ireland, a horse slaughterer of Baker Street. The threat of proceedings brought about a spectacular improvement in the state of Ireland's premises.

THE LOCAL BOARD WINS THROUGH

Despite the set-backs, Enfield Local Board of Health did have a solid core of achievement to its credit by 1870. It had the nucleus of a sewerage and water supply which was extended and improved during the remainder of the nineteenth century.

Many of the problems that beset Enfield can be attributed to inexperience on the part of Board members and the lack of suitably trained staff. It is indeed remarkable that the Enfield Local Board of Health achieved as much as it did in its early years in view of its staffing problems – a senile road surveyor, a semi-literate farmer as surveyor and a dubious solicitor as clerk. When confronted with difficulties the Board ultimately faced up to them and persisted in its efforts. This at least is to the credit of the Board members. At Hitchin, the Local Board, faced with the problems of a badly constructed sewer system and a waterworks that leaked like a sieve, simply dissolved itself and handed back the responsibility to the Vestry. This might have been an easy way out for Enfield too, but, fortunately, the members of the Enfield Local Board were made of sterner stuff. An element of stability and continuity was provided by James Meyer as Chairman. He must take at least some of the credit for the fact that these early setbacks did not prove mortal.

Made in Enfield

TRADITIONAL INDUSTRIES

Market gardening was for generations one of the biggest employers in Enfield, the proximity of London ensuring a ready market for fruit and vegetables. The final extinction of this industry took place only after World War II, when London's air pollution took its toll and the land was worth more for building.

To the north of Enfield Town the back gardens of the Willow Estate still contain a large number of fruit trees left over from the orchards that once covered this area. The glasshouses, once full of ripening tomatoes, cucumbers and hothouse grapes, have mostly disappeared, leaving behind nothing but telltale shards of glass in the soil. Of the glasshouses that supplied the demand for house-plants and garden plants, rather more has survived. A substantial remnant hangs on at Crews Hill as garden centres, though most of the plants sold are now grown elsewhere.

An old windmill of uncertain date stood at the top of Windmill Hill, operated by several generations of the Robinson family. It was eventually demolished as late as 1904. (The author's grandfather, born in 1890, used to pass it daily on his way to and from school.) The Ponders End Mill, once powered by the River Lee, has remarkably

72. Remains of the Bell Nursery in the Hertford Road opposite Albany Park, awaiting demolition in 1955.

survived to the present day. The buildings, which include a delightful miller's house, date from the late eighteenth century, but it is a strong possibility that a mill was on site as far back as Domesday. Work on the George V Reservoir (opened 1913) cut off the source of waterpower and the machinery

71. The Enfield Windmill c.1900. It was demolished in 1904.

is now electrically powered. The mill has been owned by the Wright family for over a century and they have managed to strike a delicate balance between the needs of conservation and the demands of running a business in a competitive world.

Tanning was once a major industry in Enfield and was already established by late medieval times. It was probably at the height of its prosperity during the seventeenth century. One tan yard survived close to Enfield Town in Silver Street as late as 1831. The loss of this industry should not be mourned: tanning is essentially a dirty trade, smelly, highly polluting and incompatible with the amenities of an urban area.

Brickmaking was common in the Lee Valley until recent times. With building stone difficult to come by immediately north of London, and supplies of brickearth readily available, brick was made and used from an early date. Essex was a centre of activity, with brick being widely used by the late medieval period. It was used to good effect especially in church towers, examples of which are at Nazeing and Epping Upland, and nearer to home, a fine specimen of early sixteenth century brickwork can be seen in the south porch of All Hallows Church, Tottenham. The earliest surviving dateable brickwork in Enfield is in the original building of Enfield Grammar School (*c*.1590).

Two types of brick were manufactured locally:

74. *Ponders End Mill, c1900. Now electrically powered, the mill is still in use and is Enfield's oldest industrial building.*

soft reds and yellow stocks, both of which can be seen in local buildings. There were extensive brickfields on the Edmonton border in Bush Hill Park and also in Southbury Road and Lincoln Road. The last Enfield brickworks, Gabriel & Co. (formerly W.D. Cornish) survived in Hoe Lane until 1976. There were also large brickfields in the Bury Street area of Edmonton and in the White Hart Lane area of Tottenham. Many defective bricks, which had been over-fired or fused in the kilns, were sold off cheaply and used to build garden walls.

73. A brickworks on the Enfield/Edmonton border c.1910.

THE CRAPE FACTORY

Messrs Grout and Baylis opened a factory for dyeing and finishing black crape in 1809 at the junction of South Street and Scotland Green, Ponders End. The firm prospered particularly in the Victorian period when mortality rates were high and mourning customs were elaborate and rigid.

An interesting picture of the factory workforce emerges from a notebook kept by Rev. John Fuller Russell, Vicar of St. James, Enfield Highway (1841-1854). Russell made a point of visiting the workers in their homes and made notes of his impressions of them. The workforce, as in most textile factories, was predominantly female and not particularly well paid. The few men who were employed were mostly in a managerial/supervisory capacity and were significantly better paid. Here are some typical extracts from Russell's notebook.

Ann Carrington
Married. Many years at factory. Turns a reel to dry crape 9/- per week. No allowance in sickness. Slovenly ignorant woman. Never attends church. Has 3 daughters – all badly conducted persons before marriage. Little hope of amendment. Lives in Goat Lane [i.e. Queensway].

Betsy Nicholls
Married. Employed in making up the packets of crape at 8/- per week. No allowance in sickness. Has a little girl supposed to be illegitimate – 4 years old. Does not attend school. Has an infant since marriage. Never attends church or meeting house. Lives nearly opposite the White Hart. Has been employed in the factory since a child. Her mother lives with her – character doubtful

James Broomham
Labourer. 17/- per week. Very quiet, well-behaved man about 22 years of age. Lives with his brother. Writes a remarkably fine hand. Do for a Sunday school teacher?

David Conyard
Black dyer. Good servant. Civil man. 20/- per week. His wife a pieceworker – average 7/- per week. He attends the meeting house, but not very regularly. His children attend the meeting school. Perseverance here might do some good.

Later in the century, as death rates declined and funeral customs became less elaborate, sale of crape declined. The factory closed in 1894 with the

75. *A scene at Messrs. Grout and Baylis' crape factory which operated between 1809 and 1894.*

76. The Royal Small Arms Factory at Enfield Lock, showing the canal basin, formerly the millhead.

machinery and some of the skilled workers being taken to another factory owned by the same company at Great Yarmouth. The remaining workers were discharged, causing considerable distress in the Ponders End area. During the following winter St Matthew's Church nearby in South Street ran a soup kitchen and the Enfield Highway Co-operative Society distributed free bread to the unemployed. However, the factory building was soon acquired by United Flexible Metal Tubing Ltd (see below).

THE ROYAL SMALL ARMS FACTORY

The products of this factory have reached every corner of the world. It had its origins in the demand for weaponry created by the Napoleonic War and the inability of the private small arms companies to meet that demand. The factory was constructed by the War Office on a then remote site at Enfield Lock beside the River Lee, which was used to supply water power for the machinery and transport of both raw materials and finished weapons. The factory buildings were designed by John By, a Royal Engineers' Colonel, with some assistance from the eminent civil engineer, John Rennie. (By is little known in Britain, but was to achieve fame in Canada, where he was responsible for building the Ottawa and Rideau Canals and he founded the settlement of Bytown, which was to form the core

of Ottawa.) The factory came into production in 1816, just too late to affect the outcome of the Napoleonic War.

Initially it manufactured muskets, swords and bayonets, but the muskets soon gave way to the Enfield Rifle, a greatly superior weapon. A shortage of weapons caused by the Crimean War of 1854/5 resulted in the factory being reorganised on mass production lines utilising methods and machinery pioneered in the USA at the famous Springfield Armoury, Massachusetts. A prominent part in this reorganisation was played by the eminent engineer, Sir Joseph Whitworth, whose patent screw threads were in general use throughout British industry.

The Martini-Henry Rifle was produced at Enfield and used to good effect in the Zulu War of 1879. This was superseded by the Lee Metford, which had a short life, before giving way to the Lee Enfield, which was used extensively in the Boer War. A refined version of this, the Short Magazine Lee Enfield (introduced in 1902) proved to be one of the finest military firearms of all time and was the standard British infantry weapon throughout both world wars. The factory also played a major part in the development of machine guns – the Sten and Bren were both mass-produced there during World War II.

The RSAF workers were an unusual bunch. The highly skilled nature of much of the work tended

77. *A workshop at the Royal Small Arms Factory decorated with flags and bunting to mark the Relief of Mafeking (1900).*

to create a working class elite in East Enfield and by the standards of the time pay was good. They were rather more articulate than the average working man, and it does not come as a great surprise to learn that there was a trade union established at the factory as early as 1855 and that RSAF workers were the prime movers in the establishment of the Enfield Highway Co-operative Society in 1872.

The presence of a pool of skilled labour encouraged other firms to settle in Enfield, so that the area near the Lee became industrialised. In particular, Enfield acquired a reputation for high quality engineering.

The end of the RSAF came in 1988 soon after the factory, together with other plants in the Royal Ordnance group, had been sold to British Aerospace. The famous pattern room collection, containing examples of every weapon made at Enfield, and a major piece of Enfield's industrial history, was quietly removed and is now housed at the Royal Ordnance Factory at Nottingham. The factory site, despite well publicised pollution problems, is currently being redeveloped for housing. (Readers wishing to know more about this factory should read *The Royal Small Arms Factory Enfield* by David Pam (1998).

THE GAS INDUSTRY

The Enfield Gas Company was established in 1850 to manufacture and supply coal gas in and around Enfield Town. A gasworks was built in Sydney Road, opening in 1852. In 1859 the Ponders End Gas Company commenced operations in South Street alongside the railway. The two companies eventually merged in 1879 and in 1882 gas manufacture was concentrated on the Ponders End site, the gasworks at Sydney Road being closed. The site of the latter is currently earmarked for a new Central Library. The Enfield Gas Company was taken over in 1914 by its mighty neighbour, the Tottenham and District Gas Company, which had commenced operations in 1847 with a gasworks on the Tottenham/Edmonton border at Willoughby Lane.

Immediately after World War II, the company undertook a complete rebuilding of the Ponders End Gasworks, making it one of the most up to date plants in the country. These opened in 1949, one year after the company had been nationalised. But the advent of natural gas from the North Sea meant that the plant had a working life of just over twenty years. Enfield was converted to natural gas between 1971 and 1972 and gas manufacture at Ponders End ceased, although part of the site is still used for gas storage.

78. The Ponders End Gasworks in the process of reconstruction after World War II.

ELECTRICITY SUPPLY

Brimsdown Power Station was opened in 1904 by the North Metropolitan Electric Power Supply Company, a subsidiary of Metropolitan Electric Tramways (*see p98*). It was built primarily to supply power for the tramways, but the company soon realised that there was money to be made from selling surplus electricity for domestic use. The Enfield Town area got its first electricity in 1907, supplied from Brimsdown via a sub-station in Ladysmith Road. A pioneering electric street lighting installation was inaugurated at Green Lanes, Winchmore Hill in 1913.

Initially electricity was used for lighting in place of gas, but was soon used for cooking, water heating and powering domestic appliances. Brimsdown Power Station was substantially enlarged between the wars to meet increased demand. A regular sight at Brimsdown was of complete train-loads of coal from Nottinghamshire and South Yorkshire being shunted into the power station sidings.

Brimsdown closed in 1976, for by this time power could be produced more cheaply by larger and more modern plants elsewhere. The mighty cooling towers, once one of the great landmarks of Enfield, were felled by explosive, leaving a huge gap in Enfield's skyline.

ELECTRICAL MANUFACTURING

Enfield became a major centre for the manufacture of electrical goods. The carbon filament light bulb had been invented more or less simultaneously by Thomas Alva Edison in the USA and Joseph Swan in England. Swan established the Swan Electric Lamp Co. at Newcastle in 1881. Then in 1883 the two men jointly established the Edison Swan United Electric Light Co., better known by its trade name, 'EDISWAN', opening a factory at Benwell, Newcastle and in 1886 another at Ponders End in

79. The former Brimsdown Power Station, once a major landmark on Enfield's skyline.

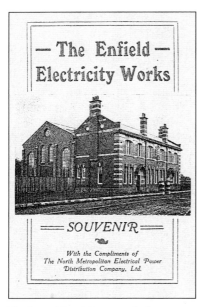

— The Enfield —
Electricity Works

SOUVENIR

*With the Compliments of
The North Metropolitan Electrical Power
Distribution Company, Ltd.*

80. *Booklet issued in 1907 to mark the commencement of domestic electricity supplies in Enfield.*

premises that had been used by the London Jute Works from 1867 until going bankrupt in 1882. The carbon filaments used in the original light bulbs were desperately fragile, and had a very short life. There was clearly a need for a more robust material, and in 1907 the company pioneered the use of tungsten filaments. The early bulbs were made of plain glass, giving a harsh light, but this problem was solved by the opal lamp (1921) and the pearl lamp (1927). Research work carried out at the factory by Dr Ambrose Fleming led to the invention of thermionic valves in 1904, one of the most important discoveries of the twentieth century. The valves, vital components of radio, television, radar and early computers, were manufactured in small numbers from 1905 and mass-produced from 1916. The company became part of Associated Electrical Industries in 1928, which in turn became Thorn AEI Valves and Tubes Ltd. in 1961. The Ponders End factory, by now increasingly unsuitable for modern electrical manufacturing, closed in 1969 and was sold a year later.

Charles Reginald Belling was a Cornishman, born at Bodmin in 1884. He served an apprenticeship in electrical engineering with Crompton & Co. of

81. *Cooling towers at Brimsdown Power Station being felled by explosive in 1976.*

82. A mass meeting of workers at Bellings in 1979. Such scenes were relatively rare as this company normally had reasonably good labour relations.

Chelmsford (later Crompton-Parkinson) before joining the staff of Ediswan at Ponders End. In 1912 he started his own company in small premises in Lancaster Road, Enfield, manufacturing electric heaters. The product range was progressively widened to include electric water heaters (1913), electric cookers (1919), and immersion heaters (1920). Additional factory space was acquired at Derby Road, Edmonton in 1913. This sufficed until the opening in 1924 of a purpose-built factory at Southbury Road which, with progressive enlargements, was to serve the company for the rest of its days. The end came suddenly in June 1992, when the company went spectacularly bankrupt. The Southbury Road site has since been redeveloped.

83. Belling electric cookers, as advertised in a catalogue of 1935.

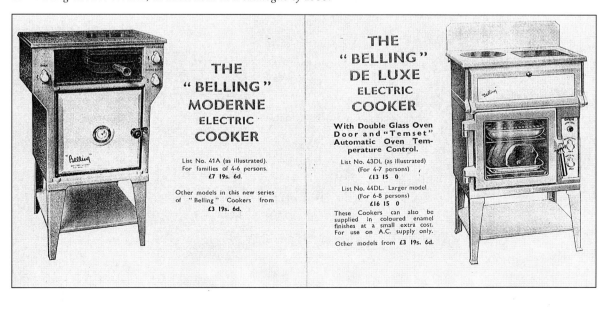

Belling-Lee Ltd. was set up in 1922 by Belling in partnership with Edgar Morton Lee to manufacture mains-powered radio sets after the commencement of BBC broadcasting. Maintenance problems caused the company to abandon these in 1924 and production was switched to crystal sets. The original factory was located at Queensway, Ponders End, moving in 1932 to new premises on the Great Cambridge Road. The company's range of products increased over the years to include fuses and fuse holders (1929), electrical gramophone pick-ups (1933), and radio aerials (1935). During World War II much of its production switched to radar components and VHF aerials for use on aircraft. In the post war years there was a huge demand for television components and the factory was progressively extended. In 1966 it became part of the Philips group and in 1991 the building was closed and sold for redevelopment.

Many other electrical firms have operated in the Enfield area. Sangamo-Weston were established in Enfield in 1921, moving to the Great Cambridge Road in 1938. They were manufacturers of electric meters and time switches. Further down the Great Cambridge Road, the Ferguson Radio Corporation commenced production in 1937, making radio sets, and later televisions. Ferguson was a major constituent of Thorn Electrical Industries, later part of Thorn EMI, a remarkable company presided over by the late Sir Jules Thorn, an Austrian-Jewish entrepreneur of somewhat irascible temperament. Various parts of the Thorn group came to be located on the Great Cambridge Road and the company was a major employer in Enfield.

ENGINEERING

One of the more unusual companies trading in Enfield was United Flexible Metal Tubing of Ponders End. Flexible metal tubing was invented in France in 1885 by Eugene Levasseur, a Parisian jeweller, who used the techniques that he had previously employed in making coiled gold necklaces. The UK rights to the invention were acquired in 1890 by Frederick Walton who took over the former crape mill premises in Scotland Green Road (see above) soon after its closure in 1894. Business grew rapidly as new applications were

84. The foundry at United Flexible Metal Tubing, Scotland Green c.1910.

85. A workshop at United Flexible Metal Tubing c.1910. Note the belt-driven machinery.

found for the invention. Improvements in railway technology created a demand for air brake and steam heating hoses and another use was the protection of electricity cables. The company also developed an early bellows-operated vacuum cleaner. The company was taken over by the TI Group in 1969 but the factory has since closed and been redeveloped for housing.

Other engineering based companies included Meeson Bros. (later the Arlington Motor Co.) in Ponders End High Street in 1918, which built buses and coaches. The Meesons had previously acquired a grounding in engineering at the Royal Small Arms Factory. The Enfield Rolling Mills commenced operation at Brimsdown in 1924 with second hand machinery acquired from Germany as war reparations. An unusually specialised company was Berkel & Parnell Ltd. of Aden Road, which manufactured bacon slicing machines.

DECLINE AND FALL

Enfield's industries boomed during the two world wars and held up remarkably well through the depression years of the thirties. The post-war years, despite fluctuations in the economy, saw a huge demand for electrical goods and other consumer durables which was sufficient to ensure continued prosperity in Enfield. But competition from the Far East, particularly in the field of electrical goods, began to bite. In the 1980s numerous factories closed or relocated, culminating in the closure of the Royal Small Arms Factory in 1988. They leave behind a legacy of dereliction and polluted sites. Enfield's industry, even when prosperous, was neglectful in the matter of waste disposal. The author's grandfather, employed as a maintenance engineer at an Enfield factory between 1939 and 1960, regularly saw chemical waste, including cyanide, poured down a well shaft. Many of the factory sites, particularly on the Great Cambridge Road, have been redeveloped as retail complexes which, welcome though they may be, are a poor substitute in employment terms.

Paths of Righteousness: Enfield at Prayer

THE GREAT PEW DISPUTE

St Andrew's Church in Enfield Town, once the only place of worship in the parish, remains a predominantly medieval building. Although a church existed prior to the Norman Conquest, nothing remains from this period and the earliest work that can be identified with certainty is some thirteenth century masonry and a window in the chancel. The unbuttressed west tower and nave arcades date from the fourteenth century. The early sixteenth century saw both aisles rebuilt and a lofty clerestory added to the nave, thereby substantially brightening the interior, which must previously have been excessively dark. The south aisle and porch were rebuilt for a second time in brick in the 1820s.

By the mid nineteenth century the interior was cluttered with box pews which virtually filled the nave and aisles. This state of affairs was not to the liking of Rev. John Moore Heath (1808-82) who had been appointed Vicar in 1844 on the death of

86. A late 19th-century view of St Andrew's Church with the stonework still covered in plaster rendering. Maintenance of the churchyard is clearly not a new problem.

Rev. Daniel Cresswell. Heath was the great-nephew of General Sir John Moore, the hero of the battle of Corunna, and was the son of a distinguished barrister. As a supporter of the High Church wing of the Church of England, he had very definite ideas as to how worship should be conducted and how the church should be furnished. These ideas by and large did not find favour with his congregation, who regarded Heath's Anglo-Catholic tendencies with the greatest suspicion.

The issue of the church pews was to become an extraordinarily contentious one. In 1853 Heath and his Vicar's warden, David Waddington, worked at how to get rid of the old box pews. Waddington, a tough north country businessman from Manchester mill-owner stock, was chairman of the Eastern Counties Railway and Tory MP for Harwich. His business methods were totally unscrupulous and his career nose-dived in 1856 when he was ejected from the board of the railway company for embezzlement. He had lived at Adelaide House, Forty Hill since 1847.

Heath had plans for new pews prepared by the architect, James Piers St Aubyn and raised a public subscription to cover the cost of the work, but significantly, did not seek the permission of the Vestry and did not apply to the Bishop of London

87. John Moore Heath, Vicar 1844-70.

88. A late 19th-century interior view of St Andrew's Church, showing the pews installed amid such great controversy in 1854.

for a faculty. The problem was that the Enfield Vestry was dominated by a clique of local gentry hostile to Heath's brand of churchmanship, many of whom were also owners of the box pews that Heath wished to remove.

Heath struck the first blow on the night of 11/12 October 1853. A gang of workmen was hired by Waddington in Norwich and conveyed by special train to Ponders End from where they were transported under cover of darkness to Enfield Town to the church. The following morning the pews were a mass of splintered wood stacked in the churchyard and the workmen were already on their way back to Norwich.

The next Vestry meeting held on 20 October was predictably noisy, with loud calls for legal action against Heath and Waddington, but it eventually agreed to consider re-pewing the church. A committee recommended minor alterations to the Vicar's plans, that the new pews should be slightly reduced in height and that they should have doors fitted. Just as things were about to be settled a new row erupted over whether the pews were to be three feet or three feet four inches in height, and there was a demand for a poll of the Vestry voters on the issue. The poll, held in the King's Head Assembly rooms, was a rowdy and disorganised affair. A large and hostile crowd assembled – Heath's principal opponents, James Meyer of Forty Hall and Daniel Harrison of Chase Hill House, were later accused of distributing free drink to ensure a good turnout. The proceedings were further enlivened by a 'no popery' mob from Ponders End led by Thomas Brading the Ponders End postmaster, a prominent nonconformist. At one stage, the mood in the Assembly Rooms became so ugly that Heath and his curates were forced to jump through an open window and, hitching up their cassocks, ran across the bowling green to seek sanctuary in the Grammar School. The poll resulted in a crushing defeat for Heath, but in circumstances that were hardly to the credit of his opponents.

Further controversy followed at a Vestry meeting on 26 January 1854 when Heath and Waddington were accused of applying for a faculty for re-pewing the church using plans at variance with those approved by the Vestry. At a further meeting on 17 April a fight broke out between Waddington and Harrison. Waddington threatened Harrison with prosecution for assault and, having forced the latter to apologise in the most abject terms, rubbed salt into the wound by having their entire correspondence on the subject printed and circulated. The pew controversy was finally brought to a close at a Vestry meeting on 27 May, when it was reported that a faculty had been granted for the new pews. Heath agreed to abide by the terms of the faculty and not to make any alterations to the chancel.

Heath's remaining years in Enfield were far from peaceful and his incumbency degenerated into a continuing battle with his parishioners. In 1859 the Bishop of London ordered an enquiry into affairs at Enfield and later the same year a petition was sent to Parliament accusing Heath of popery. James Whatman Bosanquet of Claysemore formed the Enfield Protestant Association to oppose him.

Heath left Enfield under plea of ill health in 1865 but did not resign as Vicar until 1870. He died in 1882 in his 74th year and his body was brought back to Enfield for burial in the churchyard. The tombstone bears the text 'Lord now lettest thou thy servant depart in peace'.

Heath's successor was Rev. (later Prebendary) George Hodson, who was Vicar from 1870 until his death at the age of 87 in 1904. A staunch evangelical, he was much more acceptable to his parishioners and had a relatively trouble-free reign. But he did have a difficult relationship with the local nonconformist churches and found a doughty opponent in Rev. Henry Storer Toms, a long-serving minister of Christ Church Congregational Church in Chase Side. Much of his incumbency was devoted to protecting the Church Schools whose near monopoly of elementary education was threatened by the prospect of a School Board in Enfield (*see p87*). His political views were reactionary even by the unenlightened standards of the time. He wrote a book defending the conduct of his brother who, as a Major in the Indian Army, had been responsible for one of the worst atrocities in the suppression of the Indian Mutiny, namely the cold-blooded murder of the Mogul princes. His attitude to the working class children attending his Church schools was probably not much different from his brother's attitude to the native population of India.

89. *St James, Enfield Highway, built in 1831.*

NEW CHURCHES

As Enfield expanded, other churches were built in outlying districts. St James', Enfield Highway was built in 1831, initially serving the whole of East Enfield. In 1835 Jesus Church, Forty Hill opened, largely financed by Christian Paul Meyer of Forty Hall. The first Vicar of this church, Rev. Charles William Bollaerts, was from a rather more exotic background than most clergymen of his time. His surname is clearly of Dutch origin, but according to the 1851 Census, he was born in Demerara, South America, i.e. Guyana. (Guyana had been a Dutch colony prior to being taken by Britain during the Napoleonic War.) In 1839 Christ Church, Cockfosters was built for the extreme western fringe of Enfield, the building being financed by the Bevan family of Trent Park. (The Bevans, of Welsh origin, were a Quaker business family, partners in Barclays Bank, who had recently converted to the Church of England.) All three churches were cheaply built and are good examples of the early phase of gothic revival, exhibiting a good knowledge of detail combined with a cheerful disregard for the principles of gothic composition.

90. *Jesus Church, Forty Hill, built in 1833. The chancel has since been rebuilt and extended.*

91. *St John's Church, Clay Hill. Note the polychrome brickwork in the window heads.*

St John's, Clay Hill, was built in 1857, originally as a chapel of ease to St Andrew's, and later became a separate parish. It was financed out of his own pocket by Rev. John Moore Heath, Vicar of St Andrew's, and was built to the designs of James Piers St Aubyn. The building includes some remarkable polychrome brickwork in the window heads. In its early days the services were conducted by John Moore Heath, whose High Church practices, especially the use of candles on the altar, provoked violent confrontations with the members of the locally influential Bosanquet family.

Development in the Chase Side area highlighted the need for a church in that part of Enfield and in 1874 the church of St Michael and All Angels was built at the foot of Gordon Hill. Designed by R.H. Carpenter, the building is a serious essay in French gothic with a remarkable polygonal stone-vaulted chancel. Sadly, it was never completed and the building remains a tantalising fragment.

Ponders End, until then served by St James', Enfield Highway, got its own church in 1878 with the building of St Matthew's Church in South Street to the designs of H.J. Paull. Owing to a shortage of funds only the nave and north aisle were built initially, the chancel being added in 1901. Plans for a tower surmounted by a 112-foot spire were never implemented and the south wall of the nave still has a blocked arcade which would have opened into the south aisle had the finance been available to build it.

St Mary Magdalene Church was built at the top of Windmill Hill in 1883, an unusually sumptuous building reflecting the high social status of the area. It was built in memory of Philip Twells of Chase Side House, a wealthy banker and one time MP for the City of London. The design was by William Butterfield, one of the outstanding nineteenth-century English architects. It is a large building, prominently sited, built of stone throughout, and with a lofty pyramid spire which has become one of the landmarks of Enfield. The interior is unusually rich, with much use of coloured tiles and marble work, for which the architect was well known.

St Mark, Bush Hill Park, was built in 1892 to the

92. *St Mary Magdalene, Windmill Hill (1883), an Enfield landmark.*

designs of J.E.K. and J.P. Cutts, a large thirteenth-century style building of red brick. The tower remains a short stump surmounted by a pyramid roof, the intended spire having been abandoned through lack of funds.

For development north of Lancaster Road, St Luke's Church was built in Browning Road overlooking Hilly Fields; consecrated in 1900, it was completed in 1906. The architect was James Brooks, one of the more able nineteenth-century church architects, and St Luke's is a characteristic work, a large well-proportioned building in an austere thirteenth-century style. The first Vicar, Rev. Vincent Travers Macy, an Anglo-Catholic, suffered much harassment from 'no popery' agitators within the parish.

St George's, Freezywater, was completed in 1906, replacing a temporary corrugated iron building which continued in use as a church hall. It is a large red brick gothic building again designed by the Cutts brothers and bears a strong resemblance to their earlier work at St Mark's, Bush Hill Park.

St Paul's, Hadley Wood, a small building in Camlet Way opened in 1911, replacing temporary premises in the grounds of a nearby house, St Ronan's. It was enlarged by the addition of a chancel in 1936. Although well supported and

serving an affluent area, it has never become a parish church in its own right and remains technically a chapel of ease to Christ Church, Cockfosters.

St Peter and St Paul, Ordnance Road was built in 1928 to replace the former Royal Small Arms Factory Chapel, which had closed in 1922. The building was wrecked in 1944 in a V1 incident, which also did extensive damage to the neighbouring Chesterfield Road School. The present building dates from 1969, at which date it became a parish church, having previously been a chapel of ease to St James', Enfield Highway.

At Grange Park a temporary building was replaced by St Peter's Church in Vera Avenue; this was under construction when World War II broke out and was consecrated in 1941. Designed by C.A. Farey, it is a simple brick building in a vaguely classical style. The furnishings include a marble baluster font formerly at the long-demolished City church of St Katherine Coleman.

St Giles' Church, a simple modern building, opened in Bullsmoor Lane in 1954 as chapel of ease to Jesus Church, Forty Hill. After a promising start, support waned and the church eventually closed, the empty building being destroyed by fire and the remains demolished.

93. St Peter and St Paul, Ordnance Road, soon after consecration in 1928. The building was wrecked in 1944 by a V1.

94. *Enfield Town's first Roman Catholic church, built in London Road in 1901.*

ROMAN CATHOLICISM

After the Reformation Enfield contained no major Catholic families to act as a focal point for resistance. The discovery of the Gunpowder Plot in 1605 led to a wave of anti-Catholic hysteria and one of the houses searched was Whitewebbs, which had been used by the conspirators. The house had been visited by the Jesuit priest, Father Henry Garnet, who was subsequently arrested, tortured and executed, although he was almost certainly innocent of any involvement in the plot.

In 1705 there were known to be two Catholic families in Enfield: those of Robert Leeson at Forty Hill and William le Hunt at Scotland Green, Ponders End. The latter managed to run a school for Catholic boys in conditions of semi-secrecy, later moving to Edmonton where his activities continued. During the eighteenth century conditions for Catholics improved and after the failure of the Jacobite rebellions of 1715 and 1745, they clearly no longer represented a security threat. Restrictions on their activities were gradually relaxed, culminating in full emancipation in 1829.

The numbers of Catholics in north London were boosted by the arrival of French royalist refugees fleeing the French Revolution in 1789. One group settled in Hampstead, establishing a chapel (St Mary, Holly Place) and another settled in Tottenham, building a chapel in Queen Street close to White Hart Lane. This chapel, the direct ancestor of the present St Francis de Sales Church in

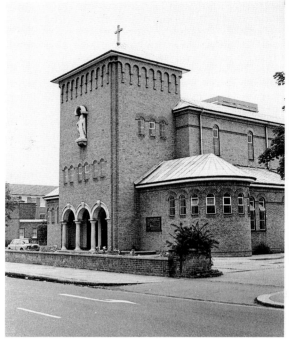

95. *Our Lady of Mount Carmel and St George (1958) replacing the previous church bombed in 1940.*

Tottenham High Road, was to play a key role in the revival of Roman Catholicism in the surrounding area. A turning point in its fortunes came with the disastrous Irish Potato Famine of 1845/8 which resulted in large scale Irish immigration to the British mainland.

Enfield's first Catholic church since the Reformation, a very simple affair, was consecrated by Cardinal Wiseman in 1863. It was replaced by a permanent church built on an adjacent site in London Road in 1901. Sadly, this building had a very short life, being destroyed by a landmine in November 1940. The present church of Our Lady of Mount Carmel and St George, a brick building in a Byzantine style, dates from 1958.

Catholics in eastern Enfield used a Catholic church at Waltham Cross, but by the late nineteenth century numbers had grown sufficiently to justify the building of a small chapel in Alma Road. Ponders End became a separate parish in 1912 and the present church of St Mary in Nags Head Road was built in 1921. This church offers extensive facilities for the large Italian community that has settled in Enfield since World War II.

Catholics in the north-west corner of Enfield use the Benedictine church of Christ the King, standing just inside the former Southgate boundary at

Bramley Road. The Church of Our Lady of Walsingham in Holtwhites Hill began as the chapel of the former St Joseph's Home, a Catholic orphanage run by the Sisters of Mercy. First registered for public worship in 1964, the church was completely rebuilt in 1987, following closure and demolition of the orphanage.

CONGREGATIONALISTS AND PRESBYTERIANS

Congregationalists developed from the Independents of the seventeenth century. The Baker Street Chapel, originally Baptist and later Presbyterian (*see p21*), was by the mid nineteenth century in the hands of Congregationalists. It was rebuilt in a sumptuous classical style in 1862, but by the early years of the twentieth century, the congregation was in decline and it closed in 1923.

The Ponders End Congregational Church began as a small chapel on the west side of Ponders End High Street, immediately north of the junction with Lincoln Road. The building was badly damaged by a bomb in 1940 and the remains were subsequently demolished, being replaced in 1959 by a building at College Court. The former Enfield Highway Congregational Church has not been so fortunate. Originating in the 1820s, it moved in 1873 to a new building on the Hertford Road, but closed in 1919, and is now the Co-op Hall.

97. Christ Church, Chase Side (1875), was the most important nonconformist church in late 19th-century Enfield Town.

96. Baker Street Chapel, c.1910. The site has been associated with nonconformist worship since the mid 17th century.

98. *Ponders End Chapel was bombed in 1940 and the remains subsequently demolished.*

Christ Church in Chase Side began in 1780 as a small chapel affiliated to the Countess of Huntingdon's Connexion (a Methodist splinter group), but later switched allegiance to the Congregationalists. An internal rift within the membership resulted in a large minority decamping to set up a rival chapel on an adjoining site in Chase Side. The two chapels eventually reunited in 1871 and in 1875 the present Christ Church was built, a gothic building with a tall spire.

Other Congregational churches are worthy of mention. The Lancaster Road Congregational Church originated as a mission from Christ Church, starting life in 1880 in temporary premises and moving to a permanent building in 1885. At Bush Hill Park a Baptist mission started in 1881 in a temporary building in Main Avenue. This was quickly taken over by Congregationalists who built the present church in 1910. The Cockfosters area is served by a building in Freston Gardens which opened in 1939.

In 1972 the Congregational Church merged with the Presbyterian Church of England to form the United Reformed Church and all the surviving Congregational churches in Enfield are now affiliated to this body.

The early Presbyterian chapel in Baker Street, as we noted above, was later taken over by Congregationalists. But Presbyterianism enjoyed

a revival in the nineteenth century with the arrival of many Scots people in the London area. By the early 1900s there were enough Presbyterians in Enfield to support a church and St Paul's Church was built at the junction of Church Street and Old Park Avenue. The hall was built first in 1902, followed by the church in 1907. In its heyday it was a prosperous and well-supported church, able to attract ministers of a high calibre. As might be expected, surviving membership records reveal a disproportionately large number of Scottish surnames. Losing support in modern times, it joined the United Reformed Church in 1972. A proposal for a merger with Christ Church led to protracted and ultimately unsuccessful negotiations and instead it merged with the nearby Enfield Methodist Church, now renamed Trinity Church. Their old building, now known as St Paul's Centre, is used as a public hall.

BAPTISTS

Although there had been a Baptist congregation established at Baker Street as early as 1669, this had failed within twenty years, and it was not until the nineteenth century that they took firm root in Enfield. In 1867 a group of Baptists held services in a room over the Rising Sun in Church Street, moving later that year to temporary premises in

99. St Paul's Presbyterian Church of 1907. The congregation included a large number of expatriate Scots. The building is now a public hall.

100. The original building of the Enfield Baptist Church in London Road.

London Road. These were replaced in 1875 by a permanent building which itself was replaced in 1926 by the present church in Cecil Road. (The London Road premises were sold and the site is now occupied by Woolworths.)

At Freezywater the Totteridge Road Baptist Church opened in 1868, in a building that subsequently became the church hall, the present church dating from 1875. The Suffolks Baptist Church began in 1934 as a mission to the then new housing estates in the Carterhatch Lane area. Land was acquired in 1938 for a church, but World War II intervened and the present church in Carterhatch Lane did not open until 1957.

There have been other Baptist churches not affiliated to the Baptist Union. The Emmanuel Baptist Church (a member of the Old Baptist Union) was established in 1933 in the former Baker Street Chapel vacated by the Congregationalists ten years earlier. The building, by then in poor repair and threatened by road widening, was demolished in 1977, and worship continued in the former church hall at the rear. This building has subsequently been acquired by the Enfield Evangelical Free Church.

METHODISTS

Methodism was a latecomer among the nonconformist churches, having broken away from the Church of England during the eighteenth century under the leadership of John Wesley. From its earliest days Methodism tended to fragment into smaller groups. One such group was the Calvinistic Methodists (or Countess of Huntingdon's Connexion) led by George Whitefield. Chase Side Chapel (see under Christ Church) was originally affiliated to this sect, but subsequently switched allegiance to the Congregationalists. After Wesley's death, there were further fractures in the movement and Methodism broke into several warring factions, the most important in Enfield being the Wesleyan Methodists and the Primitive Methodists. Happily, the differences were ultimately resolved in the 1930s and the various factions reunited.

In Enfield the Wesleyans were the dominant faction. In 1845 services were held in temporary premises in Baker Street, which were replaced by a brick building in Cecil Road in 1864. This sufficed until 1889 when the congregation moved to the present church at the junction of Church Street and Little Park Gardens. This building was badly damaged by fire in 1919 and had to be internally reconstructed. Now known as Trinity Church, it is run jointly with the United Reformed Church and incorporates the congregation from the former St Paul's Church opposite (see above).

Another Methodist church was founded in Ponders End in 1849 although there is some evidence of Methodism in the area prior to this date. After several moves, it settled in the High Street in 1931 where it remains to this day. Elsewhere in East Enfield the Ordnance Road Methodist Church started life as a small brick chapel in Grove Road. This moved in 1879 to a temporary building in Ordnance Road, which was replaced by a permanent building in 1904. The latter was superseded by yet another new church in 1957, the former building being retained as a church hall.

101. *Enfield Methodist Church (now Trinity Church).*

The Primitive Methodists held open-air meetings at Chase Side in 1851. A year later services were held in a former barn in Chase Side, which was replaced by a purpose-built chapel on an adjoining site in 1858. This sufficed until 1894 when the congregation moved into a new chapel on the east side of Chase Side, immediately south of Halifax Road. Soon after the Primitive and Wesleyan Methodists reunited in 1932, the congregation merged with the former Wesleyan Church in Church Street, the Chase Side building then being taken over by the Salvation Army.

SALVATION ARMY

The Salvation Army has operated at various locations around Enfield. The site with the longest continuous activity is at Main Avenue, Bush Hill Park which has been in use since 1902. In 1924 the Army took over the former Baker Street Chapel (see above), but in 1933 moved to the recently vacated Primitive Methodist Chapel in Chase Side. They have since moved on to Churchbury Lane where they occupy a former Anglican church hall. (General William Booth, founder of the movement, lived at Hadley Wood from 1889 until his death at the age of 83 in 1912).

OTHER CHURCHES

There have been many other smaller places of worship and it is impossible to mention them all in a work of this size. However, there are two non-denominational churches of unusual importance. The Enfield Evangelical Free Church was established in Cecil Road in 1897. The building was badly damaged in 1940 by the same landmine which wrecked the adjoining Roman Catholic church in London Road and services were held in the hall at the rear of the site until the church was rebuilt in 1956. Also worthy of mention is the well-supported Brigadier Free Church in Brigadier Hill which originated in the 1890s as a corrugated iron mission hall. The present church and adjoining youth centre date from 1970.

JEWS

Unlike its neighbours, Tottenham and Southgate, Enfield has never had a large Jewish population, but there has been a Jewish presence in the area over a long period.

Ratebooks reveal that Benjamin D'Israeli (father of Isaac and grandfather of the Prime Minister) lived in Baker Street from 1782. In 1794 Hanamel D'Aguila was living close to the junction of Turkey Street and the Hertford Road. Late nineteenth century directories reveal a thin scattering of Jewish businessmen, mainly tailors and barbers, operating in Enfield. By the end of World War II a small but significant number of Jewish families had made their homes in Enfield. To cater for their needs the Enfield and Winchmore Hill Synagogue was established in a converted private house in Wellington Road, Bush Hill Park. This is a mainstream Orthodox congregation, affiliated to the United Synagogue. (Reform and Liberal Jews have access to their own Synagogues located reasonably near at hand in Southgate).

102. *The Enfield Evangelical Free Church in Cecil Road.*

103. *Enfield Grammar School c.1800, as it would have appeared in John Milne's time. Note the sheep grazing in the churchyard.*

Spare the Rod: Enfield's Schools

ENFIELD GRAMMAR SCHOOL

The oldest educational institution in Enfield has its origins in a medieval chantry established in 1462 under the will of Agnes Myddleton. The chantry was financed by income from a large estate at Benfleet, Essex, called Poynetts. The chantry priest, in between saying masses for the soul of Agnes Myddleton, soon found himself put to work teaching the boys of the parish and some sort of school was in existence by 1508. It survived the dissolution of chantries in 1547, the parishioners, showing remarkable sleight of hand, convincing the commissioners that the purpose of the foundation had been primarily educational. A schoolhouse is known to have existed by 1557, but, although this was almost certainly on the present site, it was definitely not the building that survives today. This was erected some forty years later, being under construction in 1593 and complete by 1598. It consists of two classrooms, one above the

other, plus an attic storey with dormer-windows.

The school was by then firmly established. In 1676 there was a dispute between Enfield Vestry and the then headmaster, Robert Uvedale, who was accused of neglecting the school in favour of his fee-paying private pupils. Despite resisting an attempt to eject him, Uvedale resigned, and began his own private boarding school in the nearby Manor House.

For much of the nineteenth century the school was deeply immersed in conflict. Rev. John Milne, a rather violent Scot who had been appointed headmaster in 1791, was accused in 1818 of indulging in wholesale beatings of the boys and the Vestry voted to dismiss him. Milne retaliated by bringing a court case against the Vestry, which he won decisively. He remained as headmaster until 1830 when he resigned amid accusations of irregularities in the registers.

His successor was James Emery, appointed in 1831. He too soon fell from favour with the Vestry. He was accused of neglecting his duties, an allegation which may have some substance, as in the 1839 edition of *Pigot's Directory* he is listed not only as headmaster but also the Enfield agent for the Alliance Insurance Company. In 1846 the patience

104.   A class at Enfield Grammar School in 1883.

of the Vestry ran out and Emery was dismissed. Charles Chambers was appointed to succeed him, but Emery refused to recognise the validity of his dismissal and vacate the schoolhouse. The trustees took action to eject him, but this backfired and Emery emerged victorious with £432 costs awarded to him. A tense stand off then ensued. John Sawyer, acting as Vestry Clerk in place of his father, Henry Sawyer, hinted to Chambers, that if he could raise £450 to be paid over to Emery as an inducement to vacate the school premises, the trustees would subsequently reimburse him. Chambers did as suggested and a grateful James Emery quickly moved out of the school. Sadly, the trustees declined to honour their pledge, leaving Chambers in possession of the school but hopelessly in debt.

Despite his financial situation, Chambers' early years at the school were successful and he was able to increase the numbers of pupils. Then, in 1855 he made a fatal error of judgement when, at the invitation of the Vicar, Rev.John Moore Heath, he accepted the post of Vicar's warden at St Andrews Church in succession to David Waddington. He thereby managed to embroil himself in the battle between Heath and the Vestry which had first come to a head in the pew controversy of 1853/4 (*see*

p72). The hapless Chambers found the full force of the Vestry ranged against him, culminating in 1858 in an effort to dismiss him. With the support of Heath, Chambers survived as headmaster, but the Vestry then changed tactics and attempted to drive him out by cutting off all funding, declining to carry out any repairs to the school building and even refusing to pay the school gas bills. Chambers maintained a precarious hold on the school until 1873 when this long suffering man was finally allowed to retire with some dignity on a pension of £90 per annum.

The school re-opened in 1876 under a new headmaster, William Macdonald, who was quickly replaced by William Stephen Ridewood. It was at this point that the fortunes of this deeply troubled school began to revive. Pupil numbers began to climb, a small extension was opened in 1884 and in 1893 the school took its first tentative step towards integration into the state education system, when it received its first grant from Middlesex County Council. When Ridewood retired in 1908, he was able to hand on to his successor a totally transformed school. Prior to this time, no self-respecting Enfield parents would have sent a son there if they could possibly have afforded anything better.

VOLUNTARY SCHOOLS

Voluntary schools were provided by the churches, the first attempt to provide education for working class children whose parents, in many cases, could not afford to pay for even the most basic of private schools.

In 1806 the Enfield Church School of Industry opened its doors. As its name suggests, it was a Church of England institution, its purpose being to provide a basic education for girls, mainly in domestic subjects to fit them for work as servants. The driving force behind this school was Mrs Frances Porter, wife of Rev. Harry Porter, Vicar of Enfield 1801-22.

The school was originally located in a building on the western side of the churchyard between the Grammar School and the rear of the King's Head, known rather mysteriously as the Old Coffee House. It moved in 1876 to a new building on the corner of Silver Street and Churchbury Lane. The setting up of the Enfield School Board in 1894 meant that, within a short time, free elementary education was generally available throughout the district and schools such as this became an anachronism. Nevertheless, it managed to linger on until 1909. Its building survives as offices and its funding has been diverted to the Enfield Church Trust for Girls, which provides financial assistance to girls in further and higher education.

Nonconformist children were catered for by the British Schools run by the British and Foreign School Society, an offshoot of the British and Foreign Bible Society. The Enfield British School opened in Chase Side in 1838 and soon became a well-supported and popular institution under its long-serving headmaster, Henry Wakely. Some of the pupils came from as far away as Winchmore Hill and Enfield Lock. In 1895 the managers handed over the running of the school to the newly-established School Board and it survived until 1901 when Chase Side School opened. Its old school building still survives, having been used as a public hall, a dairy, a restaurant and, finally, a pub called the Moon Under Water. There was another short-lived British School at Enfield Highway.

The National Society for the Education of the Poor in the Principles of the Established Church was generally responsible for schools attached to Anglican churches. The first two National Schools in Enfield were both located in East Enfield. St James' School opened in 1833 on the west side of the Hertford Road immediately south of the junction with Old Road. A separate boys' school was built in 1872 adjoining St James' Church, now occupied by the Enfield Highway Community Centre. The Ponders End National School (later St Matthew's) opened in temporary premises in

105. The Enfield Church School of Industry (left) in Silver Street. The building survives as offices.

106. The former Enfield British School in Chase Side photographed in 1970 when it was in use as a dairy. It is now a pub called the Moon Under Water.

1838, moving to a permanent building in South Street in 1841.

The Trent National School, funded by the Bevan family of Trent Park, opened in 1838 on a site adjoining Christ Church, Cockfosters just inside the neighbouring parish of East Barnet. A boys' school was added in 1859 in Cockfosters Road; this closed in 1938. The former schoolmaster's house still stands adjoining a garage close to the junction of Chalk Lane and Cockfosters Road.

The Enfield National School (later St Andrew's) opened in London Road in 1839, moving to a new building in Sydney Road in 1879. (The author's grandfather, Harry Ford, was a pupil here from 1895.) Other National schools included that at the Royal Small Arms Factory School (1846), Forty Hill School (1851), and St Michael's (1865) as the Holly Bush Infant School in Chase Side, the present building at the foot of Brigadier Hill being built as a boys' school in 1882. The Gordon Lane School opened on the north side of what is now Gordon Road in 1872; this closed in 1923 and the premises later used as a scout hall until demolition in 1971. (The author, briefly a member of the 4th Enfield Cubs in the mid 1950s, remembers the building as dark, cold and smelling of a mixture of damp and leaking gas.) At Enfield Wash, Ordnance Road School (later St George's) opened in 1874, moving to the present site in Hertford Road in 1936. The Bush Hill Park National School (St Mark's) opened in Main Avenue in 1882 and although it closed in 1937, the building survives as the Bush Hill Park

Library. On the rural fringe, St John's School at Clay Hill opened in 1889, but there is some evidence of an earlier school there in temporary accommodation as far back as 1858. Development in the Lancaster Road area resulted in the opening of St Luke's School in Hawthorn Grove in 1893. This had a very short life, being closed in 1911 within a year of the opening nearby of Lavender Road School. Remarkably the building has survived and is currently used as a scout hall.

A Catholic school (St Mary's) opened in Alma Road, Ponders End, moving in 1928 to the present building in Durants Road behind St Mary's Church. In Enfield Town St George's School commenced

107. Mr Easthaugh, head of the Forty Hill School, posing outside the schoolhouse with his wife and daughters.

108. *A classroom at Forty Hill School.*

operations in 1903 in Cecil Road in a building originally used as a Catholic Church (*see p78*). It moved to its present site in Gordon Road in 1939.

THE 1870 ACT

By the second half of the nineteenth century, it was clear that voluntary schools, even when supported by government grants, were unable to cope with the growing demand for school places. Gladstone's Liberal government therefore passed the 1870 Education Act, which contained provisions for the setting up of directly elected school boards to build and run schools in areas where there was deemed to be an insufficient provision by voluntary schools. The minister chiefly responsible for this remarkable piece of legislation was William Forster, a member of a prominent Tottenham Quaker family.

The same year saw the appointment of George Hodson to succeed John Moore Heath as Vicar of Enfield. Despite being 53 years of age at the time of his move to Enfield, Hodson was a vigorously energetic man. With Hodson, what had started as a wholly commendable zeal for Church schools, degenerated as he grew older and his arteries narrowed, into a pathological hatred of school boards and all their works. He was determined that no school board should ever be established in Enfield and, for more than twenty years, he succeeded.

Hodson was a formidable fund raiser and was able to finance the building of a remarkable number of the Church of England schools mentioned above. This was achieved as Enfield's population was entering a phase of rapid expansion, rising from 16,054 in 1871 to 31,536 in 1891. As the majority of the newcomers were of child bearing age, the rise in the number of children was correspondingly greater.

109. *Prebendary George Hodson, Vicar of Enfield 1870-1904, who did his utmost to prevent a school board being set up in Enfield.*

In fact, despite Hodson's best efforts, throughout this period there was a shortfall in school places. This the worthy Vicar managed to conceal from the Board of Education by supplying it with figures which he must have known were inaccurate. However, eventually the point came where the shortfall reached a level that no sleight of hand on his part could disguise.

The situation was particularly serious in Bush Hill Park where a group of aggrieved parents, mainly nonconformists and Liberals, began writing letters to the Board of Education protesting about the state of affairs there. At first the Board's officials failed to take the protest seriously, but then an MP asked a Parliamentary question concerning school places in Enfield. Strangely, it was not the local MP, Colonel Bowles, who asked the question, but Francis Allston Channing, Liberal MP for East Northamptonshire, a man with no known connection with Enfield. (But it may be significant that Channing was well-known for his support of railway trade unions in their fight to curb the excessive hours worked by signalmen. The population of the poorer part of Bush Hill Park included a considerable number of railwaymen, many or most of whom would have been union members.) As a result of Channing's intervention, the Board of Education began to take complaints from Enfield seriously. In August 1893 the Board announced that there was a shortfall of 519 school places. This was disputed by Hodson, who questioned the figures, claiming that only 250 new places were needed. The Vicar tried and failed to raise money by public subscription to provide more places. Then came a shock statement from the War Office, announcing its intention to close the school at the Royal Small Arms Factory. Thus it came about that in January 1894 the Board of Education issued an order for the establishment of a School Board in Enfield.

The first School Board election took place in March 1894 and was hotly contested, with fourteen candidates fighting for nine seats. The result was not what Hodson had hoped and prayed for. His Church Party (i.e. Church of England/Conservative) took three seats and the Progressives (i.e. Liberals) took three. The remaining three seats went to independents, whose sympathies lay by and large with the Progressives. One of these was Rev. C.E.J. Carter, (who topped the poll in the election), curate-in-charge of the Royal Small Arms Factory Chapel, a Christian Socialist with High Church leanings and no friend of Hodson. Although Hodson was allowed (out of a mistaken sense of deference) to become chairman, the new board was dominated by the Progressives and the dominant personality was George Spicer, a wealthy paper manufacturer living at Dunraven, a large house on The Ridgeway. He was a Congregationalist, a leading member of Christ Church, and in politics a Radical Liberal, and also a friend of John James Ridge, Enfield's formidable Medical Officer of Health. His brother, Sir Albert Spicer, was a prominent Liberal MP. After the second School Board election in 1897, Spicer displaced Hodson as chairman, and continued to hold this office until the Board was disbanded.

Almost immediately the Board took over the running of three existing schools: the British School in Chase Side, the Royal Small Arms Factory School, and a school at Botany Bay of obscure origin. All three buildings were in need of replacement. The Board's first new school opened in Main Avenue, Bush Hill Park in 1896 which, within a short time, was oversubscribed, and the building had to be enlarged in 1899. The architect was G.E.T. Lawrence, who had previously worked for the Tottenham School Board. The Enfield School Board was clearly satisfied with Lawrence's work, for he was to design all the Enfield elementary schools built between this time and the outbreak of World War I. His work compares very favourably with the harsh barrack block buildings erected by the Edmonton School Board at the same time.

Other new schools followed quickly. Chesterfield Road School, serving the Enfield Lock area, opened early in 1897, allowing the closure of the

110. *George Spicer, chairman of the Enfield School Board, 1897-1903.*

former Royal Small Arms Factory School. Later the same year Alma Road School opened, serving Ponders End. In 1901 Chase Side School was built in Trinity Street and the former British School opposite (of 1838 vintage and grossly overcrowded) closed.

THE 1902 ACT

In 1902 Balfour's Conservative government passed an Act by which school boards were abolished and their powers transferred to education committees attached to local authorities. Voluntary schools were given access to public funding for the first time, but in return were placed under the control of the new committees. Enfield Education Committee took over in 1903 with George Spicer as its chairman, an office he held until 1907. Responsibility for secondary education was placed under the Middlesex Education Committee.

The school building programme continued. Southbury Road School opened in 1905, Eastfield Road School in 1909, and Lavender Road School in 1910. In 1912 a new school opened in Southbury Road, named after George Spicer who had died the previous year, and in 1914 a new Botany Bay School opened in East Lodge Lane. By 1914 school provision in Enfield had reached a level that was to be adequate for years to come and no more schools

111. *Class group at Bush Hill Park School, the first school completed by the Enfield School Board (1896).*

112. *Empire Day at Chase Side School in the 1920s.*

were to be erected for another twenty years.

Brimsdown School in Green Street opened in 1939 and Merryhills School was at an advanced stage of construction when World War II broke out; by special permission it was completed and it opened in 1940. Suffolks School in Brick Lane (1934) and Albany School in Bell Lane (1939) were built as senior elementary schools, in fact the prototype for post-war secondary moderns. In 1920 the Enfield Central School opened in improvised premises in what had been the senior department of George Spicer School. In 1939 Durants Special School opened at Old Road, run jointly with the Edmonton Education Committee. (This had begun in 1920 as the Nassau House School in a converted private house on the same site. It was one of the earliest special ESN schools to be built anywhere in the country.)

Grammar schools were under the control of Middlesex Education Committee. Facilities at Enfield Grammar were considerably improved in 1924 when Enfield Court was purchased from the executors of Colonel Sir Alfred Somerset for use as a lower school. Further extensions at the main building, including a new hall, were completed shortly before the outbreak of World War II.

A brand new girls' grammar school, Enfield County, opened at Holly Walk in 1909. The building, designed by H.G. Crothall, the Middlesex County Architect, is a fine example of the arts and crafts style, strikingly similar to the former Southgate County building in Fox Lane, Palmers Green. However, the choice of site in close proximity to Enfield Grammar, may have been unwise – many illicit liaisons have taken place over the years in and around the adjoining churchyard.

THE 1944 ACT

The wartime 1944 Education Act was a remarkable piece of legislation that shaped English education for more than half a century. Education powers were concentrated in the hands of county councils, but large districts, such as Enfield, were granted a degree of autonomy. Central authority rested with the Middlesex Education Committee, but Enfield, as an excepted district within the terms of the Act, had its own education committee exercising delegated powers. In practice the delegation was more theoretical than real, as Middlesex tended to keep a tight hold on the purse strings.

The most substantial change was in the separation of primary and secondary education and the abolition of elementary schools. The more academically gifted pupils continued to transfer at the age of eleven to grammar schools, but for the less gifted, who would previously have remained at elementary school until leaving at the age of four-

teen, a completely new type of school, the secondary modern, was introduced. Another type of school allowed under the Act was the bilateral or comprehensive school. (Middlesex opened a pioneering comprehensive school, Mount Grace at Potters Bar, as early as 1952.) Fees which had previously been charged for grammar school education to all except scholarship pupils were abolished.

Enfield's first secondary modern schools were by necessity improvised in what had been the senior departments of elementary schools. Later, purpose-built secondary moderns were built in Churchbury Lane (Chace Boys, 1956) and in Rosemary Avenue (Chace Girls, 1962). Another co-educational secondary modern was improvised at Theobalds, a large eighteenth-century house owned by Middlesex County Council. A secondary modern for Roman Catholic boys, the Cardinal Allen School, was opened at Enfield Road in 1962. Albany School and the senior department at Suffolks became fully-fledged secondary moderns.

Enfield Grammar School continued as before, the buildings enlarged before World War II being more or less adequate. At Enfield County the 1909 building needed some refurbishment after World War II bomb damage and a new block was added to the north, including a new gymnasium. A new boys' technical grammar school, Ambrose Fleming School, opened at Enfield Highway in 1962, the successor to the junior department of the former Ponders End Trade School of 1911.

In the early postwar years there was a large surge in the birth rate largely caused by returning servicemen marrying and starting families. This necessitated another school building programme. Enfield's first postwar primary school was Carterhatch (1949). This was followed by Prince of Wales (1950), Grange Park (1951), Honilands (1953), Worcesters (1954), Capel Manor (1958), and Hadley Wood (1965). Class sizes, although smaller than pre-war, were by modern standards huge. (The author was a pupil at Worcesters School in Goat Lane between 1954 and 1960 in a class of 41 pupils.)

THE COMPREHENSIVE REVOLUTION AND AFTER

In April 1965 Middlesex County Council was abolished and its education powers passed to the newly created London boroughs. The London Borough of Enfield comprised Enfield and the neighbouring districts of Edmonton and Southgate and in the first election, held in 1964, political control, by the narrowest of margins, went to the Labour Party.

Enfield's long-serving and highly respected

Education Officer, Eric Pascal, retired at the time of the merger and thus it came about that the post of Chief Education Officer went to Douglas Denny, Edmonton's Education Officer since 1958, with the former Southgate Education Officer, Maurice Healey as his deputy. These two men had the difficult job of making a single team out of the staffs of the three former divisional executives plus some staff transferred from Middlesex.

The dust had barely begun to settle when Anthony Crosland, Education Minister to Harold Wilson's Labour government, issued an instruction to all local authorities to prepare plans for the reorganisation of secondary education on comprehensive lines. Enfield Council decided to comply and Douglas Denny found himself with the task of transforming Enfield's secondary schools, working closely with the Education Committee chairman, Councillor Alfred Tanner and the chairman of the Education Development Plan Sub-Committee, Alderman Mrs Gladys Jay.

The plan was drawn up in great secrecy during the winter of 1965/66 with little serious attempt at public consultation, and the details that leaked to the press merely served to increase the fears of parents with children at grammar schools. The 1966 General Election was called during this period and Iain Macleod, Conservative MP for Enfield West, made the most of this issue, referring in a speech to 'petty doctrinaire dictation by the socialist council of Enfield'. The message clearly hit target, as Macleod maintained his majority almost unchanged, whilst elsewhere the Conservatives suffered a heavy defeat.

There were reports in the local press that many teachers, significantly mostly from grammar schools, were opposed to the changes. In March 1966 there was a protest march to Enfield Civic Centre of some 400 pupils, mainly from Enfield Grammar, Enfield County, Edmonton County, Latymer and Ambrose Fleming. Parents' meetings at Enfield Grammar and Enfield County asked the council to think again. April 1966 saw the formation of the Joint Parents' Emergency Action Committee under the able leadership of Ralph Harris of Parkgate Crescent, Hadley Wood. (Harris, now Lord Harris of High Cross, a right wing economist and General Director of the Institute of Economic Affairs, was subsequently to become a leading economic guru of the Thatcher era.)

Fuller details of the plans were published in June 1966. They involved wholesale closure of the more unsatisfactory secondary moderns, most of them improvised after the 1944 Act in former elementary school premises, but also recommended for closure the highly successful Enfield Central School. Albany School, which hitherto had had separate boys' and girls' schools on the same site, was to become fully co-educational, as was Ambrose Fleming School. Kingsmead School in Southbury Road, then under construction, was to open as a comprehensive school incorporating pupils from the George Spicer Central School, Bush Hill Park Mixed and Ponders End Girls, all of which were marked down for closure. Enfield County was to merge with Chace Girls and, most controversial of all, Enfield Grammar was to join up with Chace Boys. Suffolks Secondary Modern was to close and the building become a Church of England secondary school. St Ignatius, a leading Roman Catholic boys' grammar school, then about to move from Stamford Hill to a building then under construction at Turkey Street, Enfield, was to merge with Cardinal Allen School.

The plans dismayed Ralph Harris, who characterised the makeshift joining of schools up to a mile apart as 'Mr Denny's patchwork plan'. Perhaps even more significant was an editorial in the *Enfield Weekly Herald*, a newspaper previously well disposed to the scheme. Noting that the full plan was yet to be published, it spoke of 'a conspiracy of silence' and stated that 'questions have been answered evasively'.

In August 1966 the foundation governors of Enfield Grammar voted unanimously to oppose the scheme, the council appointed governors (in the majority) having previously voted equally unanimously in favour. In November a petition of 10,000 signatures against the scheme was presented to Parliament by local MPs Iain Macleod and Anthony Berry. In December, Education Minister, Anthony Crosland, rejected the council's scheme, the point at issue being schools on split sites. A revised scheme, involving the appointment of separate heads of lower schools, was approved in February 1967.

As the dispute moved towards a climax, feelings ran high and it became increasingly personalised. Councillor Tanner had dog excrement pushed through his letterbox and Alderman Mrs Jay, an elderly widow living alone and badly disabled with arthritis, received abusive and threatening phone calls.

The Joint Parents' Action Committee now resorted to the law with strong support from local resident, Ross McWhirter, co-founder of the *Guinness Book of Records*, and financial backing from parents and Old Grammarians including Edgar Morton Lee, a millionaire local businessman and proprietor of Belling and Lee. The court case hinged on the issue of statutory notices by the council as required by the 1944 Act. These had been issued for those schools that were to close. However, in the cases of schools which were not

Court stops 'illegal' school plan

By our Education Correspondent

Parents and ratepayers in the London borough of Enfield yesterday won a plea in the Court of Appeal for a temporary order which will keep eight schools outside the borough's comprehensive education scheme, due to start on September 7.

The court ruled that the council acted illegally in ceasing to maintain eight schools it was statutorily bound to maintain and re-establishing new schools, without giving notice to the public.

113. *One of the many national headlines for the Enfield comprehensive education dispute in 1967.*

closing but whose character was changing fundamentally, the Department of Education and Science had advised that statutory notices were not necessary and none were issued.

The Joint Parents' Action Committee were represented by Geoffrey Howe QC, then a little known lawyer with political ambitions. The judge, while agreeing that the council had indeed broken the law, refused 'on the balance of convenience' to grant an injunction on the grounds of the chaos that would be caused. The Parents then decided to appeal. In August 1967, less than a month before the scheme was due to be implemented, the case came before the Court of Appeal presided over by the then Master of the Rolls, the redoubtable Lord Denning, who had no hesitation in finding for the Parents and awarding costs against the council. Injunctions were served in respect of the proposed mergers of Enfield Grammar and Chace Boys, Mandeville, Eldon and Houndsfield, and the Higher Grade, Hazelbury and Raynham.

The council then belatedly issued statutory notices for these schools and the proposed changes were delayed until these had expired. Further trouble occurred over Enfield Grammar School.

Unable for the moment to implement the merger with Chace Boys, the council decided to split the intake for the new school equally between the two buildings. However, in the confusion, the articles of government of Enfield Grammar School, requiring the intake to be selected on the basis of ability, had not been amended. The Parents went back to court and the council was ordered to divide the intake by ability. At this point, Education Minister, Patrick Gordon-Walker, intervened, proposing to amend the articles of government of Enfield Grammar and giving only four days for objections to be heard. Further court action resulted in the time allowed for objections being extended to four weeks.

The dispute had now run its course and comprehensive education in Enfield became a reality, but some people were not entirely convinced that the scheme (as implemented) represented the true ideal of the comprehensive. The dispute had attracted vast and largely hostile attention from the media and the scheme had been almost universally vilified. The people of Enfield had witnessed the unedifying spectacle of the council being publicly humiliated in the courts and in 1968 the Enfield Labour Party paid a severe price in the form of a catastrophic defeat in the council elections, with the Council Leader, the Deputy Leader and the Education Chairman, all losing their seats.

The saddest casualty was the Chief Education Officer, Douglas Denny. The stress of this period undermined his health and he retired, a broken man, in 1974. Ironically Enfield's secondary education remains today to a substantial degree in the form that it was given by him in 1967.

The Conservatives, having taken control of the council in 1968, made no attempt to dismantle comprehensive education in Enfield but in 1970 the link between Chace Boys and Enfield Grammar was severed, the two schools regaining their independence. Enfield Grammar reverted to its original name, but did not regain its former status. Chace Boys went co-educational in 1985.

A purpose-built comprehensive, Bullsmoor School, now relaunched as Lea Valley High School, opened in 1977. Ambrose Fleming School was closed in order to free the building for use by Enfield College, and extensions to St Ignatius School on the Turkey Street site enabled the former Cardinal Allen building in Enfield Road to be closed, demolished and the site sold. Ironically, housing development on the former Highlands Hospital site has now made the provision of a new secondary school in the Worlds End Lane area a matter of some urgency. Another casualty was the Botany Bay School in East Lodge Lane; this has been closed and the building converted for use as a private house.

Into the New Century: 1880-1914

ADMINISTRATIVE CHANGES

The Enfield Local Board of Health functioned until the end of 1894 and for all but a few months of its life, its chairman had been James Meyer of Forty Hall, who died in June of that year. By then great changes had taken place. In its early days, the Board had been dominated by the gentry and James Meyer was the natural choice for chairman. By the 1880s the Board was increasingly influenced by tradesmen and businessmen with the gentry largely sidelined, but Meyer, possibly out of deference, remained as chairman until his death.

In the Board's 44-year existence, viable systems of water supply and sewerage had been installed through much of the parish, as had gas street lighting. Building control was in place, ultimately forming the basis of the modern planning system. Public Offices had been set up at Little Park, Gentleman's Row, which had been purchased for £4,000 in 1888. This building was to be the principal local government building in Enfield until the opening of the first stage of the Civic Centre in 1961. It is currently used as the Register Office.

The powers of the Board were inherited by Enfield Urban District Council, set up under the 1894 Local Government Act. For electoral purposes Enfield was divided into wards which ensured that each area had its own councillors and no one district could dominate the new authority in the way that Enfield Town had. Significantly, the first chairman of the council was John Josiah Wilson, a prosperous market gardener. The gentry had had their day.

Another administrative change had taken place in 1870 with the establishment of the Enfield Burial Board. With St Andrew's Churchyard virtually full and parts of it becoming a health hazard, action was clearly called for. The Board acquired a large tract of land near the top of Lavender Hill which was laid out as a cemetery in 1872. The work was carried out under the supervision of Thomas J. Hill, who also designed the two chapels. The Burial Board subsequently laid out another cemetery at Enfield Highway adjoining St James' Churchyard. The Board was wound up in 1920 when its functions were taken over by Enfield UDC.

RAILWAY DEVELOPMENT

New railway lines helped to stimulate growth in the Enfield area. Both the Great Eastern and the Great Northern developed their suburban services in north London and it would appear that most

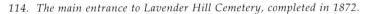

114. The main entrance to Lavender Hill Cemetery, completed in 1872.

115. *The original Great Northern Railway station on Windmill Hill, opened in 1871. The site is now occupied by Gladbeck Way.*

of their investments were sound, as almost all the lines built at this time remain in use to this day. Indeed, the only major closures have been the Great Eastern's Seven Sisters/Palace Gates line (1963) and the Great Northern's Finsbury Park/ Alexandra Palace line (1954). Within Enfield the network survives intact.

The Great Northern main line (1850) passed through the western edge of Enfield missing the main centres of population. A station was eventually opened at Hadley Wood in 1885 soon after building development had commenced in this area.

In 1859 the company opened a station at Wood Green which became a junction in 1871 when a double-track branch line to Enfield was constructed. (For an eyewitness account of the building of this line see *Winchmore Hill: Memories of a Lost Village* by Henrietta Cresswell, 1912.) Stations were at first built at Palmers Green and Winchmore Hill and, in 1880, at Bowes Park where building had just commenced. The Enfield terminus was on the south side of Windmill Hill. The station had a long island platform surmounted by a wooden awning supported on cast iron columns and, fronting the road, a two-storey structure combining a booking office and station master's house.

Initially the train service ran to King's Cross and also to Moorgate using a connection to the Metropolitan Line, which had been installed in 1863. However, increasing congestion on the approaches to King's Cross which caused delays to suburban trains, led to a connection being made from Finsbury Park to the North London Railway at Canonbury and from 1875 NLR trains from Broad Street ran to and from Great Northern suburban destinations, including Enfield. Unlike the Great Eastern, the Great Northern was far from generous in its provision of workmen's trains and, in fact, did its best to encourage lucrative 1st and 2nd class season ticket traffic. It was no accident that most of the suburban development that took place in the vicinity of its stations was middle class.

Further development of the Enfield branch line occurred so as to bypass the section of the main line where it narrowed from four tracks to two through the tunnels at Hadley Wood and Potters Bar. The plan was to extend the branch northwards through Cuffley and Hertford to rejoin the main line at Stevenage. Construction began in 1906 and involved heavy engineering work including an embankment across Chase Green, a big cutting at Lavender Hill and a massive brick viaduct to the

116. Excavation in progress on the site of Gordon Hill Station.

117. Street level buildings at Enfield Chase Station.

south of Crews Hill. It was impossible to utilise the original station at Windmill Hill, as this would have involved a level crossing, unacceptable even then, and also there would have been extensive property demolition on the plush Bycullah Estate. Instead, a new line was built, slightly to the east of the old, on a high embankment in order to gain sufficient height to cross Windmill Hill on a bridge. The first section was opened as far as Cuffley in 1910. Grange Park station was built just south of the junction of the old and new lines to serve the Old Park Grange Estate and at Enfield a new station was built on the embankment south of Windmill Hill, the old station surviving for many years as a goods depot. The other stations were at Gordon Hill, Crews Hill and Cuffley.

In 1904 the Great Northern announced plans for the electrification of their suburban lines and, at the same time, a scheme to widen the line from two tracks to four from Bowes Park to Gordon Hill which was to be the terminus of the inner suburban service. Gordon Hill Station was built with four platforms in anticipation of this. Both schemes were abandoned at the outbreak of World War I, and electrification did not materialise until 1976, 72 years after it had been promised.

118. Gordon Hill Station newly opened in 1910, with the platform surfacing apparently incomplete.

The Great Eastern Railway embarked on a vigorous programme of construction of new suburban lines after 1862. Enfield clearly deserved a much better service than was possible with the single track branch line and the roundabout route via Stratford. A new line was built via Bethnal Green, Hackney Downs and Seven Sisters to Lower Edmonton. Here it joined the original 1849 branch line which was then upgraded to double track between this point and Enfield Town. The new line opened in 1872, at first using the old terminus at Shoreditch, but from 1874 services were diverted to the new City terminus at Liverpool Street. At the same time, a line was built from Hackney

Downs to Walthamstow and Chingford (1873) and another was built from Seven Sisters to Palace Gates (1878). Of the three lines, only the latter failed to find lasting prosperity.

Concern about the extensive demolition of working class housing to make way for the Liverpool Street extension induced Parliament to insert into the Act for building the line a clause requiring the company to run workmen's trains at the cheap fare of 2d. return. The cheap fares applied to both the Enfield and Chingford lines. This facility encouraged a huge working class settlement up both sides of the Lee Valley with large population increases in Walthamstow, Tottenham and Edmonton. In Enfield the effect was less but nonetheless significant and much working class housing from this period still survives in the Bush Hill Park, Chase Side and Lancaster Road areas. Chase Side clearly marks the boundary between Great Eastern suburbia and Great Northern suburbia. To the east, in such streets as Gordon, Halifax and Manor Roads, can be found workmen's cottages that would not look out of place in Tottenham or Edmonton. To the west, the splendours of the Bycullah Estate and The Ridgeway have more in common with the plusher parts of Hornsey or Palmers Green.

Traffic on the new line built up rapidly. A station opened in 1880 on the Edmonton border at Bush Hill Park, where the builders were developing a new suburb. As the end of the century drew close,

119. Enfield Town Station, as rebuilt in 1872, in time for the opening of the new direct line.

overcrowding, especially on the workmen's trains, became a a serious issue and in Edmonton matters came to a head in 1899 with violent clashes between workmen and railway officials, and the formation of the Edmonton Workmen's Train Association. (For a fuller account of this see *Southgate and Edmonton Past* by Graham Dalling, 1996).

A station on the Lea Valley Line was opened at Brimsdown in 1884 and further improvements were promised with plans for an Edmonton and Cheshunt Line, now better known as the Southbury Loop. This opened in 1891. The route was double track throughout, running between Bury Street Junction on the Enfield Line and Cheshunt on the Lea Valley Line. Stations were built at Southbury Road (originally called Churchbury), Turkey Street (misleadingly called Forty Hill), and Theobalds Grove. Apart from a few peak hour through trains to Liverpool Street, the line had a shuttle service between Cheshunt and White Hart Lane where connections were made with the Enfield trains. Traffic remained fairly sparse and the builders showed little interest in developing around the new stations. In 1908 disaster struck, when a new electric tramway along the Hertford Road to Waltham Cross siphoned off most of the passenger traffic. The company withdrew the passenger service in 1909 and, apart from a brief revival during World War I and the occasional main line diversion, there were no regular passenger trains again until 1960.

121. Churchbury Station (now Southbury) on the Edmonton/Cheshunt Line. Apart from a brief revival during World War I, this station did not see regular passenger trains between 1909 and 1960.

TRAMWAYS

In 1881 the North London Suburban Tramways Company opened a horse tramway from Stamford Hill to Lower Edmonton with a depot sited at Tramway Avenue. The following year an extension northwards along Ponders End High Street to just south of the junction with Southbury Road was constructed. Just before it was opened to the public in 1882, it was passed as safe by Major-General C.S. Hutchinson, the Board of Trade Inspector who, in 1878, had passed as safe the origi-

120. Forty Hill Station (now Turkey Street) prior to closure in 1909.

122. Electric tram in Ponders End High Street en route to Waltham Cross.

123. Tram track nearing completion outside The George in Enfield Town, 1909.

nal Tay Bridge which was to collapse in a storm eighteen months later, taking a complete train with it. Enfield's first tramway was duly opened, but does not appear to have generated vast amounts of traffic, for by May 1883, the company abandoned plans for a further extension along the Hertford Road to Waltham Cross.

Business at the southern end of the line was brisker, In 1885 an extension was opened along Seven Sisters Road to Finsbury Park and from a new junction at Manor House a line was built along Green Lanes to Wood Green, opening in 1887. The company then made a fateful decision to introduce steam traction. The horses gave way to steam trams, miniature steam locomotives with the moving parts skirted to protect other road users. Unfortunately, the new vehicles proved to be too heavy for the lightly laid track, resulting in a spate of broken rails. The noise caused horses to bolt and top deck passengers were showered with smuts and cinders. Problems with their steam trams brought about the bankruptcy of North London Suburban Tramways and the routes were taken over by North Metropolitan Tramways Co. which promptly abandoned steam and reverted to horses. The section north of Tramway Avenue was abandoned at this time.

In 1901 Metropolitan Electric Tramways Ltd took over North Metropolitan Tramways and began a

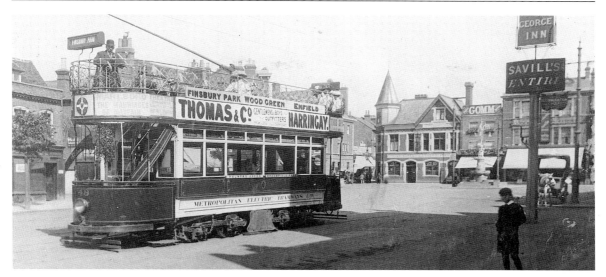

124. A tramcar outside The George soon after opening in 1909.

programme of electrification and new construction. In 1904 routes from Finsbury Park to Tottenham (Seven Sisters Corner) and to Wood Green via Manor House were electrified. A year later electric trams were extended through Edmonton to Tramway Avenue. From here the tracks were quickly installed along Hertford Road, reaching Freezywater in 1906 and Waltham Cross in 1908.

Extension beyond Wood Green was initially delayed by some bridge strengthening required in Green Lanes, Palmers Green, but once this was completed, the tramway reached Winchmore Hill in 1907. The tramcars could not manage the steep gradients and bends on the old main road over Bush Hill and so the obstacle was ingeniously bypassed, partly by upgrading existing residential roads (Park Avenue and Village Road) and partly by new construction (Ridge Avenue). The tramway reached Enfield Town in the summer of 1909, at a terminus outside The George.

The final section of Enfield's tramway network came in 1911 in the form of a branch from Ponders End to Enfield Town along Southbury Road. The trams used a temporary terminus a short distance to the east of Enfield Town Station, pending the widening of the junction of Southbury Road and The Town. The intention was to link the two tramways and, indeed, a short section of track was laid from outside The George pointing towards Southbury Road. However, by the time Southbury Road had been widened the days of the trams were numbered and the spur was never completed.

POPULATION GROWTH

The effect of improved transport facilities can be seen in population statistics. In the latter part of the nineteenth century Enfield's population grew rapidly. In 1881 it was 19,104, only about ten thousand more than in 1851. But there were sharp increases thereon: 31,356 in 1891, 42,738 in 1901, and 56,338 in 1911, though this rate of growth was still less than in Edmonton.

PUBLIC HEALTH

Enfield's more gradual growth was to its advantage, for it largely avoided the twin problems of jerry building and overcrowding which so bedevilled Tottenham and Edmonton. This is reflected in the annual reports of the Medical Officer of Health for Middlesex from 1889 onwards. Enfield was, generally speaking, either average or slightly better in most respects. Some extracts from the report of 1900 serve as illustration. The birth rate for the whole county stood at 27 per 1,000 population, as did Enfield's. (Edmonton had the highest birth rate in Middlesex with 34 per 1,000 and Tottenham was not far behind with 30.1, the lowest figure among the Middlesex urban districts being Hornsey with 19.1.) The county figure for infant mortality was 146 deaths per 1,000 live births, the Enfield figure standing at 145. Edmonton had 187 and Tottenham 173, with Hornsey at 102. Thus by the end of the nineteenth century Enfield had acceptable public health standards. Much of the credit for this must go to the highly efficient Medical Officer of Health, John James Ridge (*see p102*).

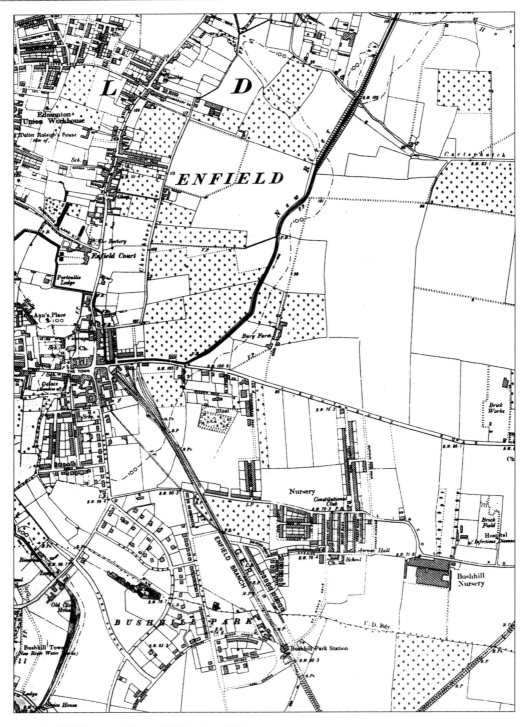

125. *Enfield Town and Bush Hill Park in 1897.*

THE BUILDERS MARCH ON

A good deal of new housing was constructed during this period. Some of the developments, such as the Bush Hill Park, Bycullah and Old Park estates, were of a high standard, but others were somewhat less prestigious and jerry building was by no means unknown.

In October 1881 houses on the Cedars Estate, Brigadier Hill, were found to have badly constructed chimneys, inadequate foundations and insufficient height between floors. Houses under construction on the Woodlands Estate (north of Lancaster Road) in 1883 had walls seriously out of perpendicular with badly bonded brickwork. In 1886, when an Enfield Local Board surveyor made a surprise visit to a building site at Standard Road, Enfield Lock, he caught the workmen mixing mortar with what appeared to be stable sweepings.

The 1897 Ordnance Survey map shows that Enfield had grown substantially, with the biggest changes occurring at Bush Hill Park, The Ridgeway and Lancaster Road.

At Bush Hill Park development had taken place since the late 1870s when work on Wellington Road, Village Road and Private Road was well advanced. This was a mainly middle-class area which, in its early days at least, had a distinct arty / crafty flavour. To the east of the railway a separate artisan suburb grew up in the Cardigan Estate, The Avenues and St Mark's Road.

Along The Ridgeway were the Bycullah Estate (1879), Old Park Estate (1880), Glebe Estate (1880) and Uplands Park Estate (1884). This area was solidly middle class, but at the bottom of Windmill Hill the Shirley Lodge Estate (Shirley Road and Station Road) had a distinctly artisan flavour according to the census of 1881.

North of Enfield Town the first houses in St Andrew's Road had been built from 1884 and work was about to start on Fyfield Road. This was a lower middle class area. Slightly to the north, Canonbury Road and Churchbury Road were intended for the artisan class. The Lancaster Road area had seen tremendous changes with the Woodlands Estate, the Birkbeck Estate, the Cedars Estate and the Laurel Bank Estate all developed from around 1880. This was predominantly an artisan area with a 'poor but respectable' flavour.

On the south side of Southbury Road building had taken place in Percival Road (1885), Fotheringham Road (1892) and Bertram Road. This area had a similar ethos to the artisan part of Bush Hill Park which lay immediately to the south.

Ponders End had seen rather less in the way of change. The Lincoln House Estate (Lincoln Road and Derby Road) had been built up from 1872 and Derby Road especially had a lower middle class flavour that has still not entirely vanished. Falcon Road (1885) was largely complete and Durants Road (1888) and Nags Head Road (1890) were still under construction.

Along the Hertford Road houses had been built or were under construction in Carterhatch Road (1890), Riley Road (1872), Ingersoll Road (1873), Albany Road (1890), Connop Road (1889), Holly Road (1889) and Oakhurst Road (1890) and also in Allandale Road. Along Ordnance Road construction had taken place in Standard Road (1886), Ashton Road (1889), Catherine Road (1891), Raynton Road and Chesterfield Road. This area had a large proportion who were employed at the Royal Small Arms Factory.

Development was interspersed with market gardens and farmland and only in parts of Enfield

126. *A house in Bush Hill Park from a sale catalogue of 1878. One house of this type still stands in Wellington Road.*

127. *An early 20th-century view of Wellington Road, a middle-class development.*

Town was the landscape solidly urban. Much of the north and west of Enfield remained stubbornly rural, though at Hadley Wood, Charles Jack began to develop a largely self-contained and decidedly up-market suburb from 1882 and by 1897 large detached houses had appeared in Crescent East, Crescent West and along part of Beech Hill and building was about to start in Lancaster Avenue.

SLUM LANDLORDS

Many of Enfield's existing houses were in poor condition. Though the Local Board had dealt with many of the worst cases, examples of neglectful landlords were brought to their attention in the 1880s. An Inspector noted, for example, some cottages in Palmers Lane off Old Road, Enfield Highway, that brickwork was cracked and bulging and there was badly decayed thatch with rafters showing through; ceilings had been patched with canvas, the privies were blocked and there was no water supply. Two slum landlords frequently appear in reports before and after 1880. These were Stephen Lancaster Lucena, a wealthy solicitor living on Windmill Hill, and Ebenezer Gibbons, a prosperous fruit farmer who was also founder of the Enfield Baptist Church.

In June 1876 a house in London Road owned by Lucena was found to be in a very parlous state. The drainpipes were broken, the back of the house was boarded up, and the window frames were so loose that there was a danger of them falling into the street and injuring passers by. In May 1880, at Lancaster Terrace, a row of cottages owned by him in Phipps Hatch Lane, raw sewage was found flowing under the floorboards.

In September 1870 cottages owned by Gibbons at Baxter's Yard, Baker Street were found to have walls and roof timbers in a dangerous state and many missing tiles. The surveyor commented that they were 'deficient in almost every requisite that should constitute a home'. In July 1877 cottages owned by Gibbons at Evans' Yard, Baker Street were found to have defective roofs, floors and ceilings.

The housing problem greatly interested Dr Ridge, Enfield's Medical Officer of Health, and on more than one occasion in his annual reports he made radical proposals for dealing with it. In 1898 he proposed that Enfield UDC should build houses under the Housing of the Working Classes Act of 1890, but this suggestion fell upon stony ground and Enfield did not in fact construct any council housing until after World War I. (It is a strange irony that of the local authorities of north-east Middlesex, the only ones to build council housing before 1914 were among the least radical and most middle class – Hornsey and Southgate.)

128. Dr John James Ridge, Enfield's Medical Officer of Health 1881-1908.

DR RIDGE TAKES OVER

The Local Board, though legally obliged to appoint a Medical Officer since 1872, had evaded its responsibilities in a rather clever fashion. It came to a dubious arrangement with Dr Agar, a Ponders End general practitioner, whereby he carried out any medical work required by the Local Board on a fee basis. This worked out very much cheaper than employing a salaried Medical Officer of Health. In December 1880 the Enfield Board received a letter from the Local Government Board urging the appointment of a proper medical officer and at the same time requested an annual report for the year 1880. This latter request infuriated the Local Board members and they decided, on the grounds that the Local Government Board made no financial contribution to Dr Agar's remuneration (doubtless because of the irregular nature of his appointment), to refuse to make such a report. In June 1881 the Local Board was still of the opinion that the existing arrangement with Agar was satisfactory, but the Local Government Board pressed for a salaried medical officer to be appointed and offered to contribute to the salary. The Local Board finally gave in and decided to comply and Dr John James Ridge was appointed in September 1881. This marked the beginning of the career of one of the strongest characters to serve as a senior local government officer in Enfield.

Ridge was born in 1847 at Gravesend and was thus 34 years old at the time of his appointment. He had been in Enfield for nine years, having taken over the practice of a Dr Benjamin Godfrey at Carlton House, Baker Street in 1872. He was a deeply religious man, a Deacon of Christ Church Congregational Church for 33 years and was Superintendent of the Christ Church Sunday School. Passionately devoted to the temperance movement, he opened some tearooms in Silver Street and published luridly worded tracts on the evils of alcohol abuse. He was a staunch supporter of the Liberal Party and was a close friend of George Spicer, the Liberal chairman of Enfield School Board. His annual reports are crisply worded and give the impression of a brisk and efficient man. He died in 1908 at the age of 61 and was buried at Lavender Hill Cemetery, where the gravestone still survives.

Among Enfield's many public health problems were epidemics. In 1879 there had been an outbreak of typhoid with 100 cases and five deaths. The worst affected areas had been Bell Lane and Grove Road West in Enfield Highway, Ponders End and the Chase Side area. (It was the mishandling of this epidemic which resulted in the Local Government Board pressurising Enfield into the appointment of a salaried medical officer.) In October 1881 there was another outbreak of the disease in Ordnance Road. By 1882 the Local Board was adopting more radical measures and in May reported that the Inspector of Nuisances, Mr Monro, acting on Ridge's instructions, had fumigated a house where there had been a case of scarlet fever

129. The Enfield Isolation Hospital in World's End Lane, opened in 1900.

and had burned infected bedding. During the autumn of 1882 there was a major outbreak of scarlet fever in East Enfield with 16 deaths. Ridge took advantage of this to press for the purchase of equipment for sterilising infected clothing and bedding. During this period scarlet fever was more or less endemic among the population of Enfield. In addition there were frequent outbreaks of measles, diphtheria, whooping cough, enteric fever and summer diarrhoea as well as the occasional case of smallpox.

To prevent the spread of these diseases, Ridge pressed the Local Board to build an isolation hospital. This did not find favour with the members, who tried to shift the responsibility on to the Edmonton Board of Guardians. The Guardians, however, wrote to the Board refusing to admit any cases of infectious disease other than paupers into their infirmary. There was therefore great difficulty in finding a suitable hospital willing to accept cases of infectious disease from Enfield and eventually in July 1884 an arrangement was made with the London Fever Hospital in Liverpool Road, Islington whereby Enfield patients were accepted at a charge of 3/- a day. This was, however, an unsatisfactory stop gap.

Eventually Ridge wore down opposition and in December 1891 a temporary isolation hospital was opened in Lincoln Road. This rapidly became overcrowded and another site was acquired in Worlds End Lane where a permanent isolation hospital was opened in February 1900. Later known as South Lodge Hospital, it eventually merged with the adjoining Highlands Hospital. The remaining buildings were destroyed by fire in unknown circumstances in 1996.

SEWERAGE PROBLEMS
By 1880 most of the built up areas of Enfield had main drainage, but there were still problems on the rural fringes. The Goat Lane area of Forty Hill was still without sewer connections and in February 1880 there were difficulties with overflowing cesspools. It was not until 1898 that a new sewer drained Goat Lane and Carterhatch Lane. In 1880 an extension from the Baker Street sewer was laid along Lancaster Road to drain the Birkbeck Estate and in the same year a sewer was laid from the Bush Hill Park Estate to Ponders End High Street. The Slades Hill area was particularly difficult for geographical reasons. The initial idea was to lay a sewer along the valley of Salmons Brook to connect with the Edmonton network, but this came to nothing when Edmonton refused to co-operate. So in 1891 an ingenious compromise was devised. The effluent was gathered in a tank beside Salmons Brook and then pumped over the top of the hill

and discharged into the sewer draining the Old Park Estate to the south of Windmill Hill from where it could find its way by gravity to the Ponders End outfall.

The Ponders End Sewage Works was a frequent cause of friction between the Enfield Local Board and both the Lee Conservancy Board and neighbouring authorities. In February 1880 the Conservancy Board complained about raw sewage escaping into the East London Waterworks intercepting cut and in April 1880 threatened Enfield with legal action unless this ceased. The Conservancy Board complained again in March 1884. This was investigated by the surveyor, Mr Kitteringham, who claimed that the discoloration of the water was caused by dye effluent (presumably from Grout and Baylis' Crape Factory) and not by sewage. In November 1885 Tottenham Local Board complained about pollution of the Lee, which it blamed on Enfield.

WATER PROBLEMS

By 1880 the Waterworks was in a parlous state, with the pumps, reservoirs and mains unable to cope with the rising demand. There was a need for much capital investment to bring the system up to an acceptable standard. This seemed too much to the Local Board and in April 1882 it decided to sell off the waterworks to a private consortium, but the Local Government Board refused permission for this. In April 1885, a water tower was built on Holtwhites Hill to improve the supply to the Old Park and Glebe estates.

Additional well shafts were constructed in Alma Road from 1887 and in 1894 the Board purchased the privately owned Bycullah Waterworks, which increased the amount of water available for the western half of the parish. The Enfield Waterworks, then at its peak, became part of the Metropolitan Water Board in 1904.

In the early years of the MWB some major works were carried out in the Lee Valley. The former East London Waterworks Co. (est. 1807) had in 1893 obtained an Act authorising the construction of a chain of reservoirs along the Lee Valley – the Banbury and Lockwood reservoirs (between Tottenham and Walthamstow) were both completed in 1903. The MWB continued this programme and built another massive reservoir on the marshes between Enfield and Sewardstone. This was opened by King George V in 1913 and was named in his honour. In 1935 work commenced on the William Girling reservoir (south of Lea Valley Road), but the project was not completed until 1951.

130. Firemen picking over the wreckage after the Sydney Road fire on 5 June 1885.

THE FIRE BRIGADE

In March 1880 it was decided to form a volunteer fire brigade under Mr Kitteringham, the Local Board Surveyor. Twelve men volunteered and were provided with helmets and hatchets. At this time the fire engine in use was a hand-cranked model dating from the 1840s, which became increasingly difficult to maintain, but in July 1883, after persistent complaints from the firemen, a new engine was purchased for £398 from Merryweather & Co. of Greenwich. This steam-powered engine was capable of pumping 260 gallons per minute and could throw a jet of water 160 ft into the air, the boiler being able to raise steam within six to eight minutes.

One of Enfield's most spectacular fires occurred on 5 June 1885 at Allen Fairhead's builder's yard in Sydney Road. The fire got a good hold and spread to the neighbouring yards belonging to Messrs Patman and Herbert and the nearby pub, the Duke of Abercorn. Additional fire engines came from Edmonton, Cheshunt, Waltham Abbey, Buckhurst Hill, Leyton, Walthamstow, Highgate, Hornsey, Wood Green and Tottenham. The water mains were pumped dry and the firemen were forced to pump from the New River at Southbury Road.

PUBLIC LIBRARIES

In 1892, after a poll of ratepayers, the Enfield Local Board adopted the 1850 Public Libraries Act. A room was fitted out in the Public Offices at Little Park, a librarian appointed and books acquired by purchase and donation. The library opened in July 1894 but the accommodation soon proved to be inadequate. After a substantial donation from the Carnegie Trust a branch library was opened at Enfield Highway in 1910, followed two years later by the Central Library in Cecil Road. The latter was intended to be part of a complex of municipal buildings, which, had things gone according to plan, would have covered what is now the Library Green.

CHILDHOOD RECOLLECTIONS

The author's maternal grandfather was born in Enfield in September 1890 and died in December 1979, his memory clear to the last. His recollections provide an interesting picture of Enfield life at the close of the nineteenth century.

Harry Ford was one of ten children (four boys and six girls) all brought up in a small cottage on The Ridgeway. His father, William Frederick Ford

131. The newly built Central Library in Cecil Road in 1912.

was a bookbinder, employed as a foreman casemaker by J.M. Dent & Co. at their workshops at Great Eastern Street, Shoreditch. The family fell within the 'poor but respectable' bracket.

Shopkeepers figure prominently in his memories as formidable personalities, many acquiring nicknames. Samuel Lane was a greengrocer with a shop in Silver Street and a reputation for tightfistedness which earned him the nickname of 'split-brussel'. John Beaven, a prosperous grocer with a shop at the junction of The Town and London Road was known as 'split-currant' for similar reasons. Albert Lacey, who ran a small general shop in the front room of a cottage on The Ridgeway, was a crabby and cantankerous man. As a result of a skin complaint, one of his ears was withered and was always covered with a leather patch, earning him the nickname of 'old leather ear'. Lacey was frequently the target of children's pranks, including, on one occasion, a giant snowball manoeuvred into the shop and left to melt on the counter, and, on another occasion, a large railway sleeper propped against the shop door, followed by a handful of stones thrown at the window to entice him to open the door. James Horton, known

as 'Jerry', had a greengrocery business near the foot of Windmill Hill. He used a pony and trap to make deliveries to his customers. The pony had been left out to grass and was seriously overweight, its bulging flanks giving the impression that it was suffering from wind. As Jerry drove past, children would call out 'Hold your nose Jerry - your pony's going to fart'.

Children would regularly get themselves into pranks that would today probably result in a serious brush with the law. On one occasion Harry and his younger brother Fred came across an elderly tramp with a long white beard, who had fallen asleep beside a small fire in a field off The Ridgeway. The boys carefully laid a trail of dry grass from the tramp's beard to the fire and then stood back to watch while the inevitable happened.

Enfield in the days immediately before World War I was a place of very great contrasts, a strange mixture of ancient and modern, urban and rural, affluence and poverty. It was still at this stage more of a Middlesex town than a London suburb, but the influence of London was ultimately to prevail. London's Green Belt came too late to save most of Enfield.

132. John Beaven's grocery shop in Enfield Town. He was better known by his nickname, 'split currant'.

'Men who march away': 1914-18

The outbreak of war in August 1914 was greeted as enthusiastically in Enfield as in other parts of the country. The first impact was the immediate call-up of territorials and reservists. A detachment of the Hertfordshire Yeomanry complete with horses was briefly billeted in Enfield Town, as was a detachment of the Royal Field Artillery.

Enfield men enlisted in large numbers and served (and died) in all the main theatres of war – the casualty lists of the Middlesex Regiment and the Royal Fusiliers contain large numbers of them. The author's grandfather, Harry Ford, joined the Middlesex Regiment and, after a spell of garrison duty at Gibraltar, fought at Gallipoli (Suvla Bay) and in Egypt. Surviving a near fatal attack of typhoid, he returned to England 'unfit for overseas service' and spent the rest of the war based at Purfleet

Army Depot. His two elder brothers also served in the war, all three managing to survive.

In 1916, as the volunteers of Kitchener's Army were being uselessly slaughtered in the Battle of the Somme, Britain introduced conscription for the first time. The *Enfield Gazette* reported the proceedings of the local tribunal dealing with conscientious objectors – after more than eighty years they make very poignant reading. In May 1916 a leading Enfield nonconformist minister, Rev. William Colville of St Paul's Presbyterian Church, stunned his congregation by preaching a sermon denouncing the ill-treatment of conscientious objectors at the hands of the military authorities. It must have taken real courage to air such an unpopular view at this time.

Almost immediately after the outbreak of war Britain had to house large numbers of Belgian refugees. A contingent found its way to Edmonton, being accommodated in the former Strand Union Workhouse and in the adjoining workhouse school building in Millfield House. Other Belgians settled in Enfield. In 1915, 209 Belgians, including 71 children, were billeted in Enfield homes, looked

133. The author's grandfather, Harry Ford, off duty at Gibraltar in 1915. The dog was one of a litter of puppies born on the battlecruiser, HMS Inflexible, and was given to him by one of the ship's petty officers.

134. Part of a sermon preached by the minister of St Paul's Presbyterian church in support of conscientious objectors in 1916.

The Sanctity of Conscientious Conviction.

A PLEA FOR JUSTICE.

Preached in St. Paul's Presbyterian Church, Enfield,
14th May 1916.
by Rev. W. R. COLVILLE, M.A.

" *Thou shalt not follow a multitude to do evil* " Exodus 23-2.

Last Sunday morning I spoke about conscience, and it will clear the ground for what I have to say this morning if I briefly recapitulate what was said then.

In dealing with the subject of conscience it is necessary to point out that the word is often used to designate what would be more accurately called the moral sense, the faculty by which we know good and evil and which we use in forming all our judgments as to what is morally right and what is morally wrong.

Like every other faculty it can be misled and perverted. By listening to insidious suggestions either from without or within; by allowing the passions of the flesh or the lower instincts of the mind to overrule the dictates of the spirit; in short, by refusing to live up to the light one has, it is possible for the moral sense to be so blunted that what is black comes to be called white and what is white is called black. It is of this condition that our Lord said "If the light that is in thee be darkness, how great is that darkness!"

ENFIELD
WAR REFUGEES
COMMITTEE

Final
Re-union of
Belgians

TO BE HELD IN
The County School Hall
By kind permission of the Governors)
On Saturday, January 11th, 1919

*135. In 1915, 209 Belgian refugees were being
accommodated in Enfield.*

after by the Enfield War Refugees Committee. Most
returned to Belgium after the war. (The author is
intrigued by the possibility that eighty years after
the end of the war, a few of the children might still
be alive.)

The sinking of the Cunard Liner, *RMS Lusitania,*
by a German submarine in the Irish Sea on 7 May
1915 with the loss of 1,201 lives made an immediate
impact. There were several Enfield people on
board. Sir Frederick Orr-Lewis, a Canadian-born
businessman, living at Whitewebbs, and his man-
servant, George Slingsby, both survived the sinking, but Sir Frederick's health never fully recovered from the effect of his immersion in the Irish
Sea, and he remained an invalid until his death in
1921. An Enfield Wash nurserymen and his wife
returning from a trip to Canada, also survived, but,
being separated in the confusion, each thought the
other had drowned until they met on the quayside
at Queenstown. Not so lucky was Ronald Hubbard

NOTICE!

TRAVELLERS intending to
embark on the Atlantic voyage
are reminded that a state of
war exists between Germany
and her allies and Great Britain
and her allies; that the zone of
war includes the waters adjacent to the British Isles; that,
in accordance with formal notice given by the Imperial German Government, vessels flying the flag of Great Britain, or
of any of her allies, are liable to
destruction in those waters and
that travellers sailing in the war
zone on ships of Great Britain
or her allies do so at their own
risk.

IMPERIAL GERMAN EMBASSY
WASHINGTON, D. C., APRIL 22, 1915.

*136. A 1915 warning issued by the German Embassy in
Washington to transatlantic passengers on British ships.
Sir Frederick Orr-Lewis ignored it and sailed on the
Lusitania on what proved to be her last voyage.*

of Southbury Road, a sales representative of a
Liverpool rubber company, who was drowned. To
this day, it has never been satisfactorily explained
how one torpedo caused a very large ship to sink
in fifteen minutes. Although it has never been
officially admitted in Britain, it is almost certain
that the *Lusitania*, as well as a full complement of
passengers, was carrying a cargo of contraband
munitions from the USA. Orr-Lewis, who is known
to have been returning from a purchasing mission
on behalf of the Admiralty, must have had some
idea of the contents of the ship's cargo space on
her last voyage.

The *Lusitania* sinking sparked off a wave of anti-
German riots in London and elsewhere, usually
taking the form of attacks on businesses and property owned by Germans or people suspected of

being German. (Many of the victims were not German at all, but Jews, whose accents and foreign sounding names attracted unfavourable attention.) There were incidents in Tottenham, Edmonton and Wood Green. In Enfield, the author's friend, the late Sid Robinson (born in 1908), saw the smashed window of a barber's shop in Main Avenue, Bush Hill Park, owned by a German called Rhumbke. (For this and other recollections see *Sid's Family Robinson* by S.J. Robinson 1991.)

Contrary to expectations, the war was not over in a few months, but dragged on for four long years, and provision had to be made for treating wounded soldiers. Existing military hospitals could not cope and temporary hospitals were set up in requisitioned premises, including many Poor Law buildings. In Edmonton the almost brand new infirmary block at the workhouse in Silver Street became the Edmonton Military Hospital in 1915. This proved to be insufficient and the military authorities later took over the rest of the workhouse and erected further temporary buildings. The patients arrived by ambulance train at the low-level station at Edmonton Green from where they could easily be transferred to private cars and ambulances for the short journey to the hospital.

In Enfield the St Mark's Institute in Bush Hill Park was taken over for hospital purposes in 1916 – the conversion included a small operating theatre. Elsewhere in Enfield, Elm House in Gentleman's Row became a convalescent hospital in 1916. (The date is significant, corresponding with the huge flood of casualties from the Battle of the Somme). Further afield, other hospitals were improvised in a school building in Tottenhall Road, Palmers Green and in the mansion at Grovelands.

London suffered aerial bombardment for the first time with bombs dropped from airships (the dreaded Zeppelins) and later from aeroplanes. At first the Zeppelins roamed unmolested across London's night sky as they flew too high for the primitive fighter aircraft then in service, and the few high trajectory guns available stood little chance of hitting them. The terror inflicted on the civilian population was quite disproportionate to the amount of damage caused. However, once high-flying fighters carrying machine-guns firing incendiary bullets were in service, the day of the Zep-

137. Elm House, Gentleman's Row in use as a war hospital, with a group of soldiers posing in the doorway.

pelin was over. In the autumn of 1916 Enfield witnessed the destruction of two enemy airships. On the night of 3/4 September an airship was shot down in flames at Cuffley after dropping bombs on Ponders End High Street and Clay Hill. (The RFC pilot responsible, Lieutenant William Leefe Robinson, was awarded the VC.) Less than a month later on the night of 1 October, another airship was shot down in flames at Potters Bar. The whole of north London had a grandstand view of the dying moments of both airships. There were no survivors from the German crews.

Later in the war there were raids by German aircraft. In a daylight raid on 7 July 1917 a large formation of enemy bombers over Edmonton and East Enfield did a fair amount of damage. A bomb narrowly missed the gasworks in Angel Road and another fell close to the Ponders End Sewage Works. A woman in Ordnance Road died after being hit by shrapnel from an anti-aircraft shell.

To combat the menace from the air, anti-aircraft guns were sited around the locality. One of the most prominent was located on the other side of the Lee Valley at Higham Hill. Another was established on The Ridgeway with a searchlight station nearby in Hadley Road. Another searchlight was ingeniously fitted on the top deck of an open-top tramcar, which trundled up and down Southbury Road. Power for the searchlight was taken from the tramway overhead wires, the military authorities being charged for the electricity by the tramway company. However, the company failed to take account of the ingenuity of the searchlight crew who, from time to time, would reverse the wires so that the meter ran backwards.

Two airfields were opened locally. One was set up at Cockfosters in a field at Westpole Farm on the edge of the Trent Park Estate. Another, rather more substantial, was set up immediately south of Lea Valley Road on the marshes between Ponders End and Chingford: the site is now covered by the Girling Reservoir.

The Royal Small Arms Factory expanded considerably. The workforce increased and, despite trade union opposition, for the first time included women in large numbers. By 1915 the influx of workers there was causing a local housing shortage and some men were housed in huts erected near the factory. At Enfield Lock, as in other munitions manufacturing areas, the pubs were put under state control and their opening hours severely restricted so as to encourage sobriety and good production.

A huge munitions plant, the Ponders End Shell Works, opened in 1915 at Wharf Road between the railway line and the Lee Navigation. It had its own

138. A group of women workers at the Royal Small Arms Factory.

railway siding, remains of which were still visible as late as 1970. Other munitions plants were set up in Angel Road, Edmonton and at Tile Kiln Lane on the Edmonton/Palmers Green border.

Other local industries prospered during the war. Clothing manufacturers switched to making army uniforms and the demand for radio components resulted in a major expansion of Ediswan and the Ponders End factory of Thomas Morson and Co., where poison gas was manufactured.

The tramway along Hertford Road had difficulty coping with the extra passengers to the factories of East Enfield and taking advantage of this the Great Eastern Railway reinstated a passenger service on the Southbury Loop in 1915. It took the form of a shuttle service, using only one track, worked by a push-pull train, plying between White Hart Lane and Cheshunt. The loop line stations, still in good repair, were re-opened and supplemented by a temporary halt at Carterhatch Lane. The service was withdrawn in 1919 and the push-pull train transferred elsewhere, plying for many years between Seven Sisters and Palace Gates.

Domestic coal became scarce, particularly in working class areas and the severe winter of 1916/17 added to the misery. Sid Robinson (born in 1908) recalled the heating at the Bush Hill Park School being cut off at this time in order to save fuel.

As the German U-boats took a heavy toll of British merchant shipping, many foodstuffs also became

140. *George V on a visit to the Ponders End Shell Works.*

scarce. Sid Robinson recalled being sent by his mother to stand in queues in the hope of getting margarine, jam or potatoes – he was frequently disappointed. With potatoes in short supply, his mother tried some desperate expedients. She experimented with boiled rice, but as it was short grain and of poor quality, the results were distinctly unappetising. On another occasion she boiled maize intended for poultry food with similarly unsatisfactory results. Sid recalled seeing one of his sisters eating dog biscuits to stave off the pangs of hunger. (Ironically, as a result of the allied naval blockade the food situation in the major German cities was, if anything, worse and in Berlin,

139. *Ponders End Shell Works, 1917.*

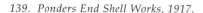

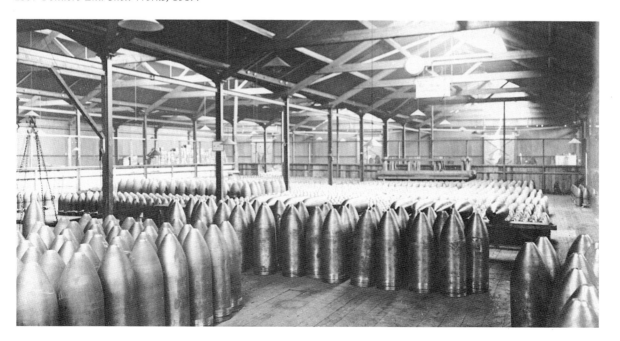

141. *Winston Churchill at the official opening of the factory canteen at Ponders End Shell Works.*

142. *Many women did what were previously men's jobs in World War I. Pictured here are post office workers leaving Enfield Town Post Office in 1915.*

by the end of the war, potatoes had become almost unobtainable, the population being reduced to a staple diet of turnips).

As the war drew to an end in 1918, an epidemic of Spanish 'flu hit Britain in three waves. There was a mild outbreak in the late spring, a severe outbreak in the autumn, and a third and final wave (less severe) early in 1919. Most of the deaths were in the second wave, which was at its peak as the war was drawing to a close in November. Many of the victims developed pneumonia, which was then largely untreatable, survival being largely dependent on the patient's physical stamina. Unusually, death-rates were highest in the younger age groups.

In Enfield 136 people died between October and December and of these 61 were aged between 25 and 45. (During the same period there were 325 deaths in Tottenham, 218 in Edmonton, 114 in Wood Green and 70 in Southgate).

The *Enfield Gazette* of 25 October reported that whole families were ill and that business had been seriously disrupted. Mail deliveries had virtually

ceased, as so many Post Office staff were sick. Many school logbooks of this period record the deaths of both staff and pupils. The logbook of Chesterfield Road Girls School, in an entry dated 11 November, records the deaths of two pupils from 'septic pneumonia'.

The official ending of the war was marked in 1919 in Enfield by a celebration in the Town Park and innumerable street parties; a war memorial was later constructed on Chase Green. Enfield Grammar School produced a Book of Remembrance (1921) with a photograph and biographical details of each old boy who had died. Possibly the most poignant relic is a hand-written war memorial book lovingly compiled by the headmaster of Chase Side School, Harry Vincent, in which he meticulously recorded not merely the names of the dead, but details of the war service of every old boy.

143. *Programme of the Eastern Enfield Peace Celebrations held at Durants Park on 21 July, 1919.*

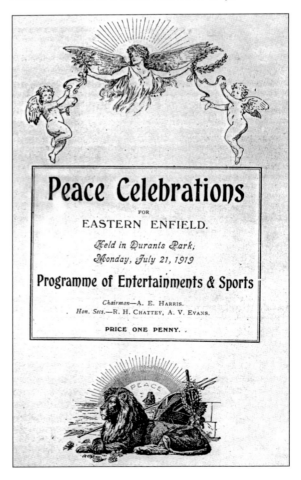

Peace Celebrations

FOR

EASTERN ENFIELD.

Held in Durants Park,
Monday, July 21, 1919

Programme of Entertainments & Sports

Chairman—A. E. HARRIS.
Hon. Secs.—R. H. CHATTEY, A. V. EVANS.

PRICE ONE PENNY.

Half-time: Enfield Between the Wars

RECOVERY

Peace brought an economic slump. The munitions factories closed and many other firms, suddenly with reduced order books, were forced to lay off workers. The huge Ponders End Shell Works closed in 1919, the buildings later being sold off piecemeal as a ready-made industrial estate. The Royal Small Arms Factory was desperately short of work and there was a proposal (not followed up) to use spare capacity at the plant to build and repair railway wagons. (At Woolwich Arsenal railway locomotives were built at this time, only to discover that the railway companies did not want them, were very reluctant to pay for them and, in any case, could build them more cheaply themselves.) However, despite these problems, Enfield's industrial base was essentially sound and the slump was no more than temporary.

At the 1921 Census, Enfield had a population of 60,738, an increase of more than 4,000 over the 1911 figure. As housing construction had largely ceased during the war, the arrival of these extra people had resulted in overcrowding, particularly in East Enfield. The 1920 Ordnance Survey map shows an Enfield which had grown substantially since the previous edition in 1897.

South of Enfield Town, the Bush Hill Park area was by now solidly built up on both sides of the railway, each side retaining its distinct character. To the west of London Road, Walsingham Road and Park Crescent were both partly built and with the break-up of the Chase Side House Estate, Cecil Road had been extended in a wide loop to join Church Street immediately east of the New River bridge, but few houses had so far been erected.

Alongside Southbury Road a fair amount of construction had taken place. To the north Sketty Road, Craddock Road, Ladysmith Road, Kimberley Gardens and Mafeking Road were built between 1903 and 1909 – the Boer War street names are an aid to dating them. To the south, much building had taken place north of Lincoln Road in Downs Road, Cecil Avenue, Burleigh Road, Falmer Road, etc. This was predominantly an artisan quarter – the author's great uncle, a plasterer by trade, settled in Sketty Road as a newly married man shortly before World War I.

East of Chase Side, Heene Road and Manor Road had both been built. Alongside Lancaster Road the Laurel Bank and the Woodlands Estates were fully developed and a large amount of building had taken place on the Birkbeck and Cedars Estates. At Forty Hill there had been some rather half-hearted attempts at development in Layard Road, Bridgenhall Road, Russell Road and St George's Road. A marvellous description of this area in the early twentieth century can be found in Norman Lewis's autobiography *Jackdaw Cake* (1985).

In Ponders End there had been development either side of the High Street since the turn of the century. To the west houses had been built in Clarence Road (1905), Northfield Road (1905), Southfield Road (1911), Suffolk Road (1909) and Oxford Road (1909). North of Lincoln Road, Kingsway started life as Station Avenue in 1908 only to be renamed in 1910, presumably in honour either of the recently deceased Edward VII or the soon to be crowned George V. To the east of the High Street building had taken place in Allens Road (1901) and Orchard Road (1906) and both Durants Road and Nags Head Road were more or less fully developed.

Elsewhere in East Enfield there was little change in the Brimsdown area, but futher north houses had been built to the south of Ordnance Road in Beaconsfield Road (1902), Rotherfield Road (1904), Uckfield Road (1903), Titchfield Road (1901), and Catisfield Road (1901).

TRANSPORT INNOVATIONS

In 1920 the Great Eastern Railway, in its last days of independence prior to merging into the London & North Eastern Railway in 1923, reorganised north-east London suburban services. The driving force behind this was its American-born general manager, Henry Thornton, assisted by his traffic manager, F.V. Russell. Unable to afford electrification, improvements were dependent upon the utilisation of existing rolling-stock.

With modifications to the track layout and signalling at Liverpool Street and at the junctions at Bethnal Green and Hackney Downs, it proved possible to introduce a ten minute interval service throughout the day on both the Enfield Town and Chingford lines. A third platform was added at Enfield Town Station at this time.

North of Cuffley, work on the completion of the Great Northern's Hertford Loop was slowed down by the shortage of manpower and materials during World War I. The project involved major earthworks, two substantial brick viaducts, and the $1^1/2$ mile Ponsbourne Tunnel immediately south of Bayford. By 1918 a single line had been laid all the way from Cuffley to Langley Junction, where the loop re-joined the main line. Although this was largely devoid of signalling equipment, it was immediately opened for freight traffic, thereby

144. *Enfield Town Station c.1925. A busy scene prior to a Boys' Brigade outing.*

helping to ease congestion on the main line, especially the double track section through the Potters Bar and Hadley Wood Tunnels. With the war over, work resumed in earnest on doubling the track, installing signalling and constructing stations at Bayford, Hertford North, Stapleford and Watton-at-Stone. The line was opened for passenger traffic in 1924, by which time the Great Northern had merged into the London & North Eastern, together with its one-time rival, the Great Eastern. (With the two lines now under common management, the former GNR station at Windmill Hill was renamed Enfield Chase to avoid any possibility of confusion with the former GER station at Enfield Town.)

Enfield Town was only marginally touched by the expansion of the Underground railway system.

145. *The site of Oakwood Station c.1930.*

A northern extension of the Piccadilly Line, from Finsbury Park to Arnos Grove was opened in 1932, reaching Oakwood (then called Enfield West) and Cockfosters the following year. (At that time Cockfosters station lay in Enfield but a boundary adjustment in 1934 transferred it to Southgate.)

The 1928 London General Omnibus Co. bus map shows just two routes operating in Enfield – the 29 (Victoria/Hadley Wood) and the 69 (Camberwell Green/Wormley). This is by no means the complete picture as in the years immediately after World War I, a proliferation of small bus companies, the so-called pirates, operated in and around Enfield. Prominent among these were Redburns of Ponders End and the Wood Green based Admiral, owned by A.T. Bennett of Winchmore Hill. There were also several very small companies in Enfield, such as GWL, run by the Lewington family of Enfield Wash, proprietors of a long established bicycle shop in the Hertford Road.

In 1933 London's buses, trams and underground railways were brought under the control of the newly-formed London Passenger Transport Board. It soon became clear that the Board was strongly biased towards buses – hardly a surprise, as its senior management was dominated by men from the former London General Omnibus Company. By this time the track of most of the North London tramways was in need of major renewal, but the power supply system was still in reasonably good order. The decision was therefore made to introduce trolleybuses, electrically powered vehicles which drew their power from overhead wires fed by the old tramway supply system. The adaptation was easily accomplished with the addition of a second wire to convey the return current which

146. *GWL was a pirate operator, run by the Lewington brothers of Enfield Wash. The picture was taken at Cecil Road, Enfield Town.*

147. *The last tramcar outside The George at Enfield Town, 1938.*

148. *Trolleybuses at the terminus at Waltham Cross.*

had formerly been routed via the running rails. Both tram routes to Enfield were given over to trolleybuses in 1938 with the solitary exception of the short branch from Ponders End to Enfield Town via Southbury Road which was completely abandoned. Most of the redundant tram track was removed for scrap during World War II.

Plans had been drawn up in 1912 for a network of arterial roads in and around London, but these were left in abeyance during World War I. Work

began on them soon after the end of the war. Prominent among these schemes was the Great Cambridge Road (A10) from Tottenham to Wormley, designed to remove through traffic from the already congested Hertford Road. Construction began at Tottenham and moved progressively northwards, the new road reaching Carterhatch Lane in 1924. The road was built with a single carriageway, but with remarkable foresight, the planners left space for a second, should it prove necessary. Work started from the Tottenham end on a second carriageway, reaching the Cambridge Roundabout by 1939. (The work of dualling the A10 through Enfield was not completed until 1965.)

East/West communications were much improved by the construction of the North Circular Road from Kew Bridge to Walthamstow where it linked up with Eastern Avenue and the Southend Arterial Road. It consisted partly of new construction and partly of existing roads upgraded. The final section, Pinkham Way, linking New Southgate and Finchley, opened in 1933.

Other road schemes from this period took rather longer to materialise. As early as 1924, there were plans for a North Orbital Road from Staines to Tilbury via Watford, St Albans, Hoddesdon, Epping and Brentwood. This was constructed sixty years

149. *The junction of the Great Cambridge Road and Lincoln Road c.1935. It then had only one carriageway and seems to have been largely devoid of traffic.*

later as part of the M25. But a 1937 plan for an extension of the A10 from Tottenham to Newington Green was abandoned.

THE GENERAL STRIKE

The General Strike of May 1926 enjoyed mixed support in Enfield. Workers at the Royal Small Arms Factory and some other Enfield factories joined it and public transport was largely brought to a halt. The London General busmen, all union members, struck, but most of the smaller bus companies, the so-called pirates, carried on working. Buses operated by Redburn's of Ponders End were stoned and another pirate operator, Admiral, was forced to take its vehicles off the road by a mass picket of its depot at Willow Walk, Wood Green. Towards the end of the strike there was an attempt to run a tram service using managerial staff as drivers with policemen riding shotgun fore and aft. Striking printers reduced the *Enfield Gazette* to a thin emergency edition and shut down completely its rival the *Enfield Weekly Herald.*

PARKS AND RECREATION

Enfield Council had already made a good start in the provision of public open space. The first part of the Town Park, formerly the grounds of Chase Side House, had been purchased for £6,750

in 1901 – further land was added in 1903. The land for Albany Park was acquired in 1902 for £3,937, the park being enlarged in 1921, 1926 and again in 1935. These were followed by Durants Park (1903), the North Enfield Recreation Ground (1907) and the Bush Hill Park Recreation Ground (1908). Hilly Fields, one of Enfield's most attractive parks, was purchased for £7,950 in 1911.

In 1920 Ryan's Field was bought to form Ponders End Recreation Ground and additional land was acquired in 1925 and 1934. Then, in 1931 Enfield UDC made its two largest acquisitions to date: the Whitewebbs Estate and the mighty King George Playing Field. Whitewebbs was purchased as a regional open space from Sir Duncan Orr-Lewis for £23,000 by Enfield UDC acting jointly with Middlesex County Council. Part of the estate was laid out as a municipal golf-course, opening in 1932. The King George's Playing Field, a huge tract of former market garden land, cost £49,600. A part in the south-east corner was leased to Enfield Football Club, which had previously played on a ground off Churchbury Lane. At the northern end, adjoining Carterhatch Lane, work began on constructing a running track and stadium – this was interrupted by World War II and not completed until 1953. A miniature golf course was laid out along the western edge close to the gateway from Ladysmith Road. Work on this was completed in 1939, but before it could be opened to the

150. Hilly Fields, one of Enfield's most attractive parks, was acquired for £7,950 in 1911.

151. *Sir Duncan Orr-Lewis, the last private owner of Whitewebbs, pictured at one of his several marriages. He sold Whitewebbs to Enfield Council for £23,000 in 1931.*

public, war broke out and it was promptly dug up for use as allotments, and no attempt was made to reinstate the golf course subsequently. (As late as 1960 one of the dressing rooms adjoining the Central Café was still labelled 'GOLF SECTION', although no golf had ever been played on this site.)

A small indoor heated swimming pool combined with public baths had been built by the Enfield Local Board in 1893 at Bradley Road, Enfield Lock. Then in 1932 an open air swimming pool was opened in Southbury Road. It was a spacious affair, laid out to the highest standards of the time, and equipped with a diving board and water chute. Sadly, it was a facility that could only be used for half the year, and in need of major renovation by the late twentieth century, it was a liability to an increasingly impecunious local authority. After a long period of closure and dereliction, the remains of the pool were demolished in 1998.

THE GOLDEN AGE OF THE CINEMA

Cinema in Enfield got off to a shaky start. The Enfield Empire opened in 1909 in a converted hall in Silver Street. Still functioning in 1917, it closed soon afterwards, the premises being subsequently acquired by the *Enfield Gazette* for a printing works. This was followed in 1911 by the quaintly named Picturedrome, which operated in a converted brewery building in Horseshoe Lane. This had closed by the end of World War I, the building then being used as a pharmaceutical warehouse.

Enfield's first purpose-built cinema was the Queen's Hall in London Road, opened in 1911. When it was rebuilt in 1928, a balcony was added and sound equipment installed. After bomb damage in 1940, it lay derelict for some years, reopening in 1947 as The Florida. Always the least fashionable of Enfield Town's cinemas, it was known locally as 'the flea pit'. It survived until 1976 and, after another long period of dereliction, eventually reopened as The Townhouse.

The Ponders End Electric Theatre, at the junction of Ponders End High Street and Lincoln Road, opened in 1913. Renamed The Plaza in 1938, it was bomb-damaged in 1940, and after lying empty for nearly fifteen years, was purchased by Enfield Council for use as a public hall. (This has subsequently been closed.)

The Rialto, Enfield's finest cinema to date, opened

152. *The Ponders End Electric Theatre (later The Plaza) opened in 1913.*

153. The Queen's Hall in London Road, opened in 1911.

in Burleigh Way in 1920. It boasted a full orchestra and a tea room and in the 1960s was frequently used for special showings of films for local schools. (The author, then a pupil at the Enfield Central School, went there to see the Laurence Olivier version of *Richard III*. As a nun led in a party of girls from the Holy Family Convent School, a raucous male voice, unidentifiable in the semi-darkness, was heard to yell 'Here comes Bat Man'.) Re-named The Granada in 1967, it survived as a cinema until 1971, and was later being used as a bingo hall. The building is currently lying empty.

The Premier opened in 1921 at the junction of the Hertford Road and Bell Lane. Apart from the installation of sound equipment in 1930, it underwent little change, leading a useful if uneventful existence until its closure in 1961. It was later used as a bingo hall, being closed and demolished in 1985.

The Savoy in Southbury Road opened in 1935. An unusually large and sumptuous building, its facilities included an organ, an orchestra and a car park. In 1962 it was renamed the ABC, the name later changing to the Canon. In its last years it was crudely sub-divided to provide a multi-screen facility, but nevertheless still managed to retain much of its original fixtures and décor. Although still well supported, it closed in 1997, when the site

was sold to Tesco for a new supermarket. Its closure and subsequent demolition effectively marked the end of the cinema era in Enfield.

HOMES FIT FOR HEROES

In 1898 Enfield's Medical Officer of Health, Dr.John James Ridge (*see p102*), had urged the building of council housing. The shortage of houses after World War I made it essential and Enfield's first 28 council houses were built at Lavender Gardens, on a site purchased for £1,250 in 1921. Soon after, on a large plot of land at the junction of Southbury Road and Ponders End High Street (Aberdare Road, Brecon Road, etc), fifty houses were built, followed in 1925 by a further 164 to a smaller design. In 1924 work began on 42 houses on the west side of Baker Street (immediately north of Rosemary Avenue). Another 34 houses were built on land in Nags Head Road and Scotland Green Road. Later schemes included thirty houses in Eastfield Road (1924), twenty houses on the Westmoor Estate at Green Street (1924), and another 28 on the Billocks Estate at Green Street (1925). In Bush Hill Park land was purchased in 1925 for £4,179 at Leighton Road, Landseer Road, Second Avenue, Third Avenue and St.Mark's Road, on which another 150 houses were built. At Enfield Highway large tracts of land in Brick Lane and Carterhatch Lane were bought between 1930 and 1931 enabling the construction of 584 houses and 25 flats. By 1939 Enfield Council had built a total of 1669 houses and 31 flats.

ALL MOD CONS

A large number of private houses were also built in the 1930s when mortgages were cheap. On the border with Winchmore Hill there was extensive development in and around Vera Avenue on the Grange Park Estate and the Piccadilly Line extension encouraged building on part of Enfield Chase. On the Southgate border John Laing & Co. developed the South Lodge Estate (Lonsdale Drive, Lowther Drive, Merryhills Drive, etc.) from 1935, and development along Cockfosters Road linked Hadley Wood to the London conurbation. In East Enfield, too, the builders were busy, as much former nursery land became available for building and to the north of Enfield Town the Willow Estate was built over former orchard land, many fruit trees remaining in the back gardens. The area south of Parsonage Lane, once known as Pennyfather's Fields, was developed as the Chase Side Estate (Parsonage Gardens, Riverside Gardens, etc). At Crews Hill a small and largely self-contained suburb grew up around the railway station and the nurseries.

The author (born in 1949) grew up on the Willow Estate in a three bedroom semi-detached house in Tenniswood Road, dating from 1938. During his early years the house remained substantially as built. Internal woodwork was mostly varnished and grained and the lower halves of the walls in the kitchen and bathroom had white ceramic tiles, giving a distinctly institutional flavour. The only heating was by coal fires in each room, but, in practise, the only room normally heated was the living room at the rear of the house, where the fire also heated the hot water. Apart from the living room, floors were covered with lino rather than carpet, relieved by the occasional strategically placed mats and rugs. The kitchen was, by modern standards, very small and instead of a fridge, had a meat safe, and instead of a washing machine, had

154. A pair of houses on the Willow Estate c.1935, pictured in a publicity leaflet. The sale price was £775 freehold.

a gas fired copper and a mangle parked conveniently outside the back door. External woodwork was normally painted cream, but some houses had the sills rather daringly picked out in red. The gardens were invariably neat, planted with sunflowers, golden rod and delphiniums. Very few people owned cars and garages were relatively uncommon – a near neighbour was the proud owner of a motor cycle and sidecar. The early residents of this road were of varied origins. At least two families came from the Hackney/Stoke Newington area and another from Shoreditch. Living more or less opposite the author was a family from Bury St Edmunds. There were also at least four Scots, including the author's father, and a Channel Islander from Jersey.

By the outbreak of World War II Enfield had grown very substantially and the built up areas had mostly attained the same configuration that they retain today. The population in 1939 was estimated at 97,410. But for the shortage of capacity of Enfield's sewer system, there would have been even more building, especially in the Clay Hill and Hadley Road areas.

'Blood, Toil, Tears and Sweat':1939/45

In November 1934, a German group of so-called 'Christian' storm troopers on a visit to Enfield took part in a service at St Paul's Presbyterian Church, provoking the *Enfield Gazette* to praise the movement as 'being of a missionary character, working within the German protestant church'. The writer of these words was closer to the truth than he realised, for Martin Luther, staunch protestant though he was, was also a rabid anti-Semite. Today it is not widely appreciated that there were elements within the British middle-class who were at the very least mildly sympathetic towards the aims of National Socialism, and particularly hostile to communists and Jews.

Sir Oswald Mosley's British Union of Fascists had considerable support in north London and there was a short-lived Enfield branch with an office in Baker Street. The movement locally was strongest in Tottenham and Edmonton, but also enjoyed some middle class support, especially in Palmers Green. It was strongly opposed by the Labour Party and particularly by the Communist Party.

When war broke out in 1939 the destruction of British cities by aerial warfare appeared to be a real possibility – recent precedents from Spain, especially the bombing of Guernica, were fresh in people's minds. With this in mind, school children and young mothers were evacuated from areas of London and other big cities thought to be in danger. In Edmonton and Tottenham, both heavily industrialised, evacuation was total. In Southgate, a residential area, there was no evacuation. In Enfield, East Enfield was evacuated and Enfield Town was not. As no compulsion was used, some parents chose not to send their children away and when the expected aerial bombardment of London did not immediately materialise, some evacuees returned home.

In April 1940 the so-called phoney war ended when German forces invaded Denmark and Norway. A month later a lightning offensive over-ran Holland, Belgium and France and by June, with

155. Bell Lane, Enfield Highway after a hit and run raid, 22 March 1944.

156. Damage caused by the London Road landmine, 15 November 1940.

157. Chesterfield Road School after a hit from a VI in the summer of 1944.

the mighty French army in ruins and the British Expeditionary Force evacuated from Dunkirk minus most of its equipment, Britain faced Germany alone.

From 13 August 1940 the Luftwaffe was unleashed against Britain, initially targeting RAF bases and aircraft factories. Locally, a large force of German bombers was intercepted by RAF fighters over the Enfield/Edmonton border. In the ensuing dogfight a German bomber was shot down over the Ponders End Sewage Works and another crashed into some glasshouses in Durants Road. On 7 September there was a massive attack on the London Docks. The flames from the burning warehouses were clearly visible in Enfield. Daylight raids continued until the end of September with RAF fighters taking an increasingly heavy toll of enemy aircraft.

From 14 November a new offensive, the so-called Blitz, was launched against London and other British cities. Extensive raids hit London night after night, causing severe damage and loss of life especially in the City and East End. This campaign ended in May 1941 when much of the Luftwaffe was moved east in readiness for the German invasion of Russia.

Though Enfield was damaged during the Blitz, it was light compared with central London. On the night of 15 November 1940 two landmines fell close to Enfield Town, one at the junction of Willow Road and Peartree Road where it flattened a row of houses, killing and injuring several people, and the other at London Road, wrecking several houses and a Roman Catholic Church. A popular local dentist, Neil Edgar, was pulled out dead from the wreckage of his home. Another landmine hit the Royal Small Arms Factory on 21 November, causing extensive damage. A bomb which fell on 30

September at the junction of South Street and Ponders End High Street wrecked the Two Brewers. Two churches, the Ponders End Congregational Church and St Matthew's in South Street, were both damaged, the former so seriously that the building was never brought back into use.

After May 1941 Luftwaffe activity over London was intermittent, as the demands of the Eastern Front took priority. In March 1944 there was a spate of German hit and run raids over London. At Enfield Highway a bomb fell in Bell Lane and in nearby Edmonton the North Middlesex Hospital was hit.

In the summer of 1944 the V1 flying bombs attacked London. Although the brunt of these was borne by south London and Kent, some of them reached north London. One fell near Ordnance Road, destroying one wing of Chesterfield Road School and the adjoining St Peter and St Paul's Church – fortunately no children were killed. Another scored a direct hit on the premises of United Flexible Metal Tubing Ltd. in Scotland Green Road.

The V1s were soon followed by the V2 rockets, which travelled faster than sound and gave no warning of their approach. One fell in Bush Hill Park on 9 December 1944, flattening a row of houses in Abbey Road and causing many casualties. (A former colleague of the author, then a pupil at Enfield Grammar School, witnessed the destruction of his family home in this incident and the death of a much-loved younger sister.) Another fell on 25 January 1945 at the top of Gordon Hill, inflicting massive damage both in that road and in nearby Lavender Hill. The last of these missiles to hit Enfield fell on 25 March 1945 at Mapleton Road, Enfield, literally slicing away the fronts of a row of houses.

Fortunately Enfield's fire service was well prepared, a brand new fire station, built to the highest

158. *Clearing up after a V2 incident at Abbey Road, 9 December 1944.*

159. *The last V2 incident in Enfield: at Mapleton Road, Enfield Highway, 25 March 1944.*

160. *Enfield Fire Service tug-of-war team, 1941/2.*

standards, having been opened on Holtwhites Hill in 1936. At the same time a street fire alarm system was installed throughout the district – domestic telephones were then a comparative rarity. The full time firemen were soon supplemented by large numbers of part-timers – the Auxiliary Fire Service. During the war, the fire brigades, previously under the control of district councils, were placed under government control as the National Fire Service. (After the war the fire service was taken over by county councils.)

A small number of full-time civil defence workers had been taken on before the outbreak of war and these were quickly supplemented by large numbers of part-timers and volunteers. Air raid wardens' posts were constructed throughout Enfield, public air raid shelters were built and large numbers of Anderson shelters were installed in back gardens. Rest centres were improvised in schools and church halls.

Enfield's hospital facilities had fortunately been augmented by the opening, shortly before the outbreak of war, of a large general hospital in the building formerly occupied by the Chase Farm School. Civilian war casualties from Enfield and elsewhere in north London were treated here and, indeed, many were to die here.

In 1940, when a German invasion seemed pos-

sible, the regular forces were supplemented by the part-time soldiers of the Local Defence Volunteers, very soon renamed the Home Guard. These units were largely manned by older men, including many World War I veterans, and some younger men, who, because of special skills, were in reserved occupations and therefore exempt from service in the regular forces. Many units were workplace-based, one such being the 56th Essex Home Guard which consisted entirely of Royal Small Arms Factory workers and had the important task of guarding the factory. This unit enjoyed the reputation of being one of the best equipped of Home Guard units and was the envy of less favoured units, who had to make do with World War I cast-offs. Fortunately, there was no German invasion and the resolve of the Home Guard was never seriously tested.

Rationing of food and other commodities was imposed but nonetheless, judging by court cases reported in the press, a black market flourished as never before. Many imported foodstuffs simply disappeared from the shops. (An aunt of the author, born in 1917, recalls trying to make a Christmas pudding using chopped prunes as a not entirely satisfactory substitute for currants and sultanas, by now unobtainable.)

In order to house those made homeless by bomb-

161. A local Home Guard contingent marching through Enfield Town.

ing, local authorities were given unprecedented powers to requisition private property. In Enfield there were many houses under construction when war broke out and not yet sold. The people who were rehoused in these properties included many bombed out of inner London, especially the East End.

As in World War I, Enfield was a major centre for the manufacture of munitions and all manner of war work was undertaken by Enfield factories. Furniture factories in Enfield, Edmonton and Tottenham were pressed into service making parts for the Mosquito bomber – this remarkable machine, one of the outstanding aircraft of World War II, was built almost entirely of wood, which had the additionally beneficial effect of rendering it largely invisible to German radar.

The numbers of working women increased, and, as many of them had young children, childcare facilities assumed major importance. Enfield Council provided day nurseries – one stood on the west side of Baker Street near the Jolly Butchers, on a site now occupied by council flats. Sadly,

progress in this field was not maintained after the war – with the transfer of day nurseries to the control of Middlesex County Council in 1948, the service was allowed to run down.

There were many prisoners of war housed in Enfield. The mansion at Trent Park was used as a special interrogation centre for officer prisoners, mainly from the Luftwaffe. The highest ranking prisoner to pass through there was General Thoma, who was captured in 1942 at Alamein. Lower ranking prisoners had more modest accommodation. A large POW camp was built on land in the south-eastern angle between Bullsmoor Lane and the Great Cambridge Road and another at the northern end of the King George's Playing Field close to Donkey Lane. (Some of the huts from the latter were still standing until c.1960.) The prisoners included both Germans and Italians. Some of the Italians, choosing not to return home after the war, settled permanently in Enfield, forming the nucleus of a large Italian community based largely in East Enfield, many of them finding work in local market gardens.

Post-war Recovery: 1945/65

HOUSING PROBLEMS

With so many dwellings damaged and destroyed, the biggest task faced by Enfield immediately after the war was to provide housing. Many families were already living in overcrowded conditions and this situation was exacerbated by large numbers of discharged servicemen. The birth rate climbed rapidly and in 1951 the population was 110,465, an increase of 40,000 on the 1931 figure.

One response was the use of prefabs, temporary prefabricated bungalows. By 1952, 347 of these had been erected on sites all around Enfield. (The author recalls seeing prefabs on sites in Hoe Lane, Ladysmith Road, Churchbury Lane and Bincote Road.) As dwellings, they were remarkably well-designed – warm, comfortable and popular with the tenants, many of whom were reluctant to move out when permanent housing became available. Unfortunately they were largely constructed of asbestos, a building material whose health risks were not then properly understood.

While the use of prefabs provided a temporary respite, work proceeded on more permanent housing. Large estates were built in Turkey Street/Bullsmoor Lane, the Manor Farm Estate, Addison Road, Hoe Lane, World's End Lane, Lavender Hill and Holtwhites Hill. The new developments consisted of houses interspersed with low-rise flats, all well designed and soundly built from traditional materials. However, the World's End Lane Estate included some prefabricated houses in Lonsdale Drive and the surrounding streets.

162. Newly completed houses at Addison Road. The design of Enfield's council housing was to vary little over the next twenty years.

Attention then turned to slum clearance and redevelopment. The results can be seen in parts of Baker Street, Lancaster Road and Ponders End High Street. Many of these developments were combined with road widening schemes.

Initially, owing to the shortage of manpower and materials, the activities of private builders were largely restricted to bomb damage repairs. The observant can still readily identify some of these sites more than fifty years later. A particularly good example can be seen in Manor Road, where some early twentieth-century workmen's cottages, destroyed by a bomb in 1940, were carefully rebuilt to the original design, but using Fletton bricks rather than the original London Stocks.

Restrictions on private building were lifted in the early 1950s. Initially, the first priority was to complete some of the developments which had been left in abeyance during World War II. John Laing & Co. resumed work on the South Lodge Estate – many houses from this period, easily distinguishable from their pre-war neighbours, are in Merryhills Drive, Lowther Drive, Lonsdale Drive and surrounding streets. Elsewhere in Enfield further expansion was largely precluded by the imposition of the Green Belt around London. This included much land in the Enfield Road/Hadley Road area which, but for World War II, would have been built upon. However, there was plenty of former market garden land, ripe for building, available throughout Enfield.

Deficiencies in Enfield's sewerage system, which had slowed down building in the immediate pre-war era, were finally dealt with. The East Middlesex Drainage Scheme was inaugurated in 1957 with the opening of the first stage of the Deephams Sewage Works at Edmonton to treat sewage from Enfield, Edmonton, Southgate and adjoining areas. Plans for this scheme had been drawn up pre-war by Middlesex County Council following on from the highly successful West Middlesex Drainage Scheme, centred on the Mogden Sewage Works at Isleworth.

TRANSPORT DEVELOPMENTS

The railways were nationalised in 1948 and in 1955 British Railways' Modernisation Plan promised electrification of the lines from Liverpool Street to Enfield Town, Chingford, Hertford East and Bishops Stortford. Work began in 1958 with improvements to the track and signalling and the installation of overhead wires. This involved the reconstruction of most bridges and Enfield Town station was completely rebuilt. The Lea Valley Line between Clapton and Cheshunt was omitted from the scheme, but it did include the long-closed Southbury Loop, which had last seen passenger trains in 1919.

163. An electric train on the Liverpool Street/Bishop's Stortford service, at Lower Edmonton in 1977.

164. The Lord Mayor of London, Sir Seymour Howard, arriving at Enfield Market Square on Charter Day, 23 May 1955.

The Lea Valley Line was eventually electrified in 1969. The first stage of the Victoria Line opened in 1968, and provided Enfield with a much more direct route to the West End via the interchanges at Tottenham Hale and Seven Sisters.

In 1959 a scheme for opening out the bottleneck on the Great Northern main line through Hadley and Potters Bar was completed with the addition of extra twin-track tunnels alongside the existing Hadley South, Hadley North and Potters Bar tunnels. The stations at Hadley Wood and Potters Bar were both rebuilt with four platforms.

Also promised in 1955 was the electrification of the Great Northern suburban services from King's Cross, but in this case, the implementation was long delayed. In 1959 diesel traction was introduced, intended as no more than a temporary interlude prior to electrification. Electrification finally became a reality in 1976 with the introduction of electric trains on to the Hertford North and Welwyn Garden City services. At the same time the inner suburban service was largely diverted to Moorgate (via the former Northern City Line tube tunnels) and the services to Broad Street and Moorgate (via the Metropolitan Widened Lines) were abandoned. The scheme was completed two years later with extension of electrification to Royston and Hitchin.

The network of trolleybuses was by now in need

of major expenditure. The power supply system, much of it a relic from the former tramways and fifty years old, was in a bad state. As trolleybuses were also regarded as a major source of traffic congestion, the decision was made to replace them with conventional diesel buses. Enfield's trolleybus services were all abandoned in 1961, but some of the masts for the overhead wires, which also carried streetlights, survived for a year or two longer.

BOROUGH STATUS

Almost immediately after the end of World War II the Labour Party took control of the Enfield Urban District Council and was to retain it until the formation of the London Borough in 1965. The Enfield Labour Party of this period was a fairly moderate middle-of-the-road affair, in sharp contrast to its more militant comrades in nearby Edmonton. The party had previously controlled the council for short periods between the wars.

Enfield became a municipal borough on 23 May 1955, when a royal charter of incorporation was presented by the then Lord Mayor of London, Sir Seymour Howard. Enfield had considered applying for borough status more than twenty years earlier, but squabbles over ward boundaries and then World War II had scuppered the original scheme. (Enfield's neighbours, Southgate and Edmonton, had become boroughs in 1933 and 1937 respectively.)

One of the first priorities was the building of new

165. *The Charter Day Lunch in the hall of Enfield Grammar School, 23 May 1955.*

offices worthy of the local authority's new status. The Council's principal offices were still in Little Park, Gentleman's Row, which had been acquired by the Enfield Local Board as long ago as 1888. It had long outgrown this building and the overflow was housed in a clutter of temporary accommodation all around Enfield Town. Fortunately, the authority had had the foresight to purchase a site in Silver Street in 1939 and this was now to be pressed into service. An architectural competition resulted in the acceptance of a design by a young architect, Eric Broughton. The first stage of the Civic Centre, incorporating a council chamber, committee rooms and some offices, was opened in 1961.

LAST YEARS OF INDEPENDENCE

Much was achieved during the period 1945-65. Enfield's public library service, after a good start before World War I, had tended to languish. No new libraries had been built since the Central Library in 1912 and in the intervening forty years the population had almost doubled. In 1948 a mobile library service was introduced to serve the outlying districts and the same year Enfield libraries became one of the very first to lend gramophone records. A branch library to serve Bush Hill Park was opened in 1948 in the former St Mark's School and this was followed by purpose-built branch libraries at Kempe Road (1957), Enfield Road (1964) and Ponders End High Street (1962).

In 1951 the Council bought the Forty Hall Estate from Derek Parker Bowles (grandson of Sir Henry Bowles). The grounds became a public park and the house a local museum, currently threatened with closure. The same period also saw a major programme of upgrading Enfield's street lighting.

166. *Ponders End Library, brand new in 1962.*

On the negative side, there was a particularly hamfisted proposal for an inner ring road to ease Enfield Town's traffic problems. The scheme was doubtless well-intentioned, but would have cut a huge swathe through St Andrew's Churchyard, Holly Walk and Gentleman's Row and would have subjected Enfield Grammar School and Enfield County School to unacceptable levels of noise and pollution. A perfectly sound row of early nine-teenth-century workmen's cottages in Church Lane was demolished to make way for the road. The scheme was vehemently opposed by the Enfield Preservation Society and in 1967 it was quite rightly rejected by the then Minister of Housing and Local Government, Anthony Greenwood.

THE END IS NIGH

In 1960 a Royal Commission on London Govern-ment recommended drastic changes in the organi-sation of London government. The London County Council and Middlesex County Council were to be abolished and replaced by a Greater London Council whose authority was to cover not only the LCC area and almost all of Middlesex, but also large slices of suburban Essex, Kent and Surrey and a small piece of Hertfordshire. Long established districts were to be amalgamated into larger units – London boroughs. The early proposals of the Royal Com-mission were substantially different from the scheme that was eventually implemented. Origi-nally, Enfield was to merge with Cheshunt, Ed-monton with Tottenham, and Southgate with Hornsey and Wood Green. But eventually, Cheshunt managed to wriggle off the hook and was to remain in Hertfordshire and Enfield was to join with Southgate and Edmonton.

The first elections for the new London Borough of Enfield were held in 1964 and were won (by the narrowest of margins) by the Labour Party. The new authority took control on 1 April 1965. Enfield's life as a municipal borough had lasted just ten years.

167. *Cottages in Church Lane which were demolished because they stood in the path of the aborted Enfield Town Ring Road.*

Literary Enfield

Enfield has been the home of many writers, including some of national and even international repute. As we have seen (*p40*), Charles Lamb was a resident of Enfield for six years.

Adrian Bell (1901-1980) was a prolific writer of novels, many of which were set in rural East Anglia. During his lifetime his work was widely read and favourably received by the critics, but since his death has been unjustifiably neglected. One of his works is of particular interest to Enfield. *A Young Man's Fancy* (1955) purports to be a novel and is the story of an adolescent boy growing up in London during World War I. The story is partly set in Enfield and includes detailed and accurate descriptions of Enfield Town, Windmill Hill and The Ridgeway. A *Kelly's Directory* of 1917 has the Bell family at Uplands Park Road and so, what was published as a novel, is in fact a very thinly disguised autobiography. Adrian Bell's son is Martin Bell, a distinguished journalist, currently (1999) serving as the independent MP for Tatton, having dispatched the disgraced Neil Hamilton in the General Election of 1997.

Sir John Betjeman (1906-1984), possibly our most popular twentieth century poet, and Poet Laureate from 1972 until his death, was a native of north London, born at Kentish Town. His family, of Dutch extraction, owned an old-established cabinet making business in Islington. Many of his poems contain references to north London. After being sent down from Oxford, Betjeman worked as a teacher at the Heddon Court School, Cockfosters from April 1929 to July 1930. Many years later he recalled this period in his poem *Cricket Master*. (Heddon Court stood in the angle between Cockfosters Road and Cat Hill and, although the

168. Heddon Court School as it was when John Betjeman was employed here.

house was demolished in the 1930s, the name survives in Heddon Court Avenue. In Betjeman's time, the house lay in Enfield, but in 1934 boundary changes resulted in it being transferred to Southgate.)

Charles Cowden Clarke (1787-1877) was a well known literary critic and author of a concordance to Shakespeare. He grew up in Enfield Town where his father, John Clarke, ran a boys' boarding school on the site of Enfield Town Station. One of his father's pupils was the young John Keats (see below) with whom he formed a lasting friendship. His wife, Mary, with whom he co-authored several books, was the daughter of Vincent Novello, founder of the famous music publishing firm. Possibly his most interesting book, *Recollections of Authors*, jointly written with Mary, contains some very useful material on both Keats and Lamb and has extensive references to Enfield.

Isaac D'Israeli (1766-1848) was a prodigiously prolific essayist and novelist, hugely famous in his lifetime, but now chiefly remembered as the father of Benjamin Disraeli. He was born in the City of London to a wealthy Sephardic Jewish family, but spent much of his childhood in Enfield, where his father owned a country house. Ford and Hodson's *History of Enfield* (1873), probably using information supplied by Benjamin Disraeli himself, states that the house was none other than the building subsequently used as a boarding school by John Clarke (see above). This story can now be refuted as Enfield ratebooks show that the D'Israelis' house stood in Baker Street, close to the junction with New Lane (Lancaster Road). It is impossible to identify the house with total certainty, but most likely it was Carlton House, later the home of Dr John James Ridge, which was demolished in 1965. Benjamin Disraeli is now known to have been a notorious source of misinformation concerning his family.

Marguerite Radclyffe Hall (1880-1943) was a novelist and poet. Openly lesbian at a time when such things were widely disapproved of, she lived between January 1919 and January 1921 with her partner, Lady Una Troubridge at Chipchase, a large house in Camlet Way, Hadley Wood. Her best known work, *The Well of Loneliness*, was the subject of an obscenity trial and, as a result, enjoyed the same celebrity enjoyed thirty years later by D. H. Lawrence's *Lady Chatterley's Lover*.

Thomas Hardy (1840-1928), the famous Dorset novelist and poet, is connected with Enfield through his second wife, Florence (1879-1937), who was the daughter of Edward Dugdale, for many years the headmaster of St Andrew's School. The Dugdale family lived in Sydney Road, moving later to River Front, opposite Enfield Town Station. Florence

169. *Isaac D'Israeli grew up in a house in Baker Street, Enfield.*

170. *Florence Emily Dugdale (wearing a straw hat) standing outside her family home at River Front in 1898.*

became a teacher, working at her father's school, where one of her pupils was *this* author's grandfather. Even before ill health forced her to give up teaching in 1908, Florence had aspirations to be a writer and she produced some not very good short stories and children's books. When and under what circumstances she met Thomas Hardy is not at all clear, but it was certainly well before the death of his first wife, Emma. What is clear, however, is that within a few weeks of Emma's death in November 1912, Florence had moved in with Hardy at his home, Max Gate, on the outskirts of Dorchester. The couple were married on 10 February 1914 at St Andrew's Church, Enfield Town. Soon after Hardy's death, there appeared a two-volume biography of him ostensibly written by Florence, but it has now been established that though it was typed by Florence, it was almost entirely ghost-written by Hardy himself before his death. Florence outlived her husband by nine years, dying at the age of 58 in 1937.

John Keats (1795-1821), the son of a City of London publican, became one of the outstanding poets of his generation but died at a young age from tuberculosis. He was a pupil at John Clarke's boarding school on the site of Enfield Town Station 1803-10 and it was here that he met the proprietor's son Charles Cowden Clarke (see above). His friendship with Clarke continued after leaving school, when, during the period 1810-13 he was articled as an apprentice to the Edmonton doctor, Thomas Hammond of Church Street, before enrolling as a medical student at Guy's Hospital.

Frederick Marryat (1792-1848) took to writing after being forced by ill-health to abandon his career in the Royal Navy. He was a prolific writer of sea stories such as *Midshipman Easy*, but is now chiefly remembered as the author of the delightful children's novel *Children of the New Forest*. Marryat was educated in Enfield at the Rev. Stephen Freeman's Academy, a boarding school at the junction of Clay Hill and Baker Street. A fellow pupil and friend was Charles Babbage, who was to become one of the finest mathematicians of his generation, still remembered for his pioneering work on calculating machines.

Walter Pater (1839-94) is remembered as an art critic and art historian and the author of a rather strange novel *Marius the Epicurean*. He was born at Poplar, where his father worked as a doctor. In 1848, the family moved to Enfield, staying ten years. The Paters lived at Chase Hill immediately west of Chase Green, but the house no longer survives, being demolished to make way for the Great Northern Railway's Cuffley extension.

171. John Keats was a pupil at John Clarke's School.

172. Frederick Marryat was a pupil at Rev. Stephen Freeman's Academy at Clay Hill.

Max Plowman (1883-1941) was a poet and literary critic, now unjustly neglected. He was born at Northumberland Park, Tottenham, the son of a wealthy brickmaker. (Thomas Plowman and Co. eventually merged into the London Brick Company.) Around 1885 the family moved to Enfield, settling in Culloden Road on the prosperous Bycullah Estate, later moving to nearby Rowantree Road. (On the opposite side of Rowantree Road, lived Thomas Plowman, Max's uncle, whose son, Tom Plowman (1875-1920), was a key figure in the establishment of the Boys' Brigade in Enfield.) During World War I Max Plowman served in the West Yorkshire Regiment and survived the Battle of the Somme. He later wrote several books of verse, including some memorable war poetry, and was also responsible for *A Subaltern on the Somme*, one of the most moving of war books. He also wrote a major work on the poetry of William Blake and was for some years editor of *The Adelphi*. His experience of war led him to embrace pacifism and, together with Canon Dick Sheppard, he played a major part in the establishment of the Peace Pledge Union, serving as its secretary 1937/8. His hopes of peace unfulfilled, he died in 1941, a deeply

saddened man, at his home near Colchester. The family home in Rowantree Road is still standing and is now the Enfield Hotel.

Osbert Sitwell (1892-1969) was a poet and short story writer, the brother of Edith and Sacheverell Sitwell. Prior to Eton, he was a pupil at the Ludgrove School at Cockfosters which he detested. He wrote about this period of his life *in The Scarlet Tree* (1946), one of his numerous autobiographical volumes. Many years later he was to return to Cockfosters as house guest of Sir Philip Sassoon at Trent Park.

Unfortunately, not all of Enfield's authors were of such high calibre. At the other end of the spectrum one finds such would-be bards as Walter Joseph Hall of Abbey Road, Bush Hill Park, who in the 1930s wrote and published two books of verse mainly about his dog. These include such memorable lines as:

> "Could you but speak, my dear
> doggie to me,
>   What endless pow wows there
> surely would be ..."

The Body Politic: Enfield MPs from 1885

Before 1832 Enfield was represented by the two MPs for the County of Middlesex (Westminster, also in Middlesex, had an additional two members). But as a result of the 1832 Reform Act, Middlesex, one of the most heavily populated counties, was given additional representation with the creation of the Finsbury, Marylebone and Tower Hamlets Divisions. In 1867 two more divisions of the county were created – Chelsea and Hackney – and in 1885 the Middlesex county constituency was broken up altogether and at the same time the Enfield Parliamentary Division was created. The Enfield constituency was a large one, including Enfield, Edmonton, Southgate, Friern Barnet, and Potters Bar. The 1918 Reform Act, as well as giving votes to women, brought about a major redistri-

bution of parliamentary seats. Edmonton became a separate seat and a Wood Green constituency was formed from Southgate and Friern Barnet (previously part of Enfield) and Wood Green (previously part of Tottenham).

The new Enfield constituency consisted of Enfield and Potters Bar. The boundary changes of 1950 split the seat into Enfield East and Enfield West, the latter still including Potters Bar. There were more changes in 1974 when the link with Potters Bar was severed when that area was transferred to the new constituency of Hertfordshire South (now Hertsmere). Other parts of Enfield West (Cockfosters, Hadley Wood and large parts of The Chase) were added to Southgate (split from Wood Green in 1950), the revised constituency being called Enfield-Southgate. The rump of Enfield West merged with Enfield East, forming a new seat, confusingly named Enfield North. Apart from some minor adjustments in 1982, the constituency boundaries remain substantially unchanged at the time of writing.

The first MP for the Enfield Division in 1885 was Viscount Folkestone (1841-1900), a Conservative, who had previously been member for South Wiltshire. His career in the House of Commons was

173. Col. Henry Ferryman Bowles, MP for Enfield 1899-1906 and 1918-22, posing on horseback outside his home at Forty Hall.

174. *William Henderson (middle row, extreme left), Enfield's first Labour MP, elected in 1923. In the centre is his much more famous father, Arthur Henderson.*

cut short in 1889 with the death of his father, resulting in his elevation to the Lords as the 5th Earl of Radnor.

In the by-election that followed, the seat passed to another Conservative, (Sir) Henry Ferryman Bowles (1858-1943). He was a local man, living at Forty Hall, the son of H.C.B. Bowles of Myddelton House and the elder brother of 'Gussie' Bowles, the famous horticulturist. Through his mother Cornelia Kingdom, he was related to the famous engineer, Isambard Kingdom Brunel. Suffering from a severe speech impediment, he found public speaking little short of purgatorial, but nonetheless he appears to have been genuinely popular in the constituency. He showed particular concern for the needs of the workers at the Royal Small Arms Factory. Many years after his death, his private life became the subject of controversy in 1985 when the Enfield-born travel writer, Norman Lewis, in his autobiography, *Jackdaw Cake* dared to suggest (probably correctly) that Sir Henry was somewhat less than monogamous.

Sir Henry's parliamentary career suffered a setback in 1906, when the election that year saw a swing to the Liberals and his seat was lost to James Branch (1845-1918), a nonconformist boot manufacturer from Bethnal Green, who had previously been a Progressive councillor on the London County Council, representing S.W. Bethnal Green. (The Progressives, an edgy alliance of Radical Liberals and Fabian Socialists dominated the L.C.C. in its early days. Their leading light was Sir John Williams Benn, grandfather of Tony Benn.)

Despite being very active on behalf of his constituents, Branch's parliamentary career was brief, losing his seat to the Conservatives in the General Election of January 1910. The successful candidate was (Sir) John Robert Pretyman Newman (1871-1947) who was of Anglo-Irish extraction, born in County Cork. During World War I, despite being over military age, he served as a major in the Middlesex Regiment. In 1918 he decided not to contest Enfield, by now shorn of Edmonton and Southgate, and stood instead at Finchley, which he held until he was unseated by a Liberal in 1924.

In Enfield the Conservatives played safe and Henry Bowles, by now aged 60, was once again elected. He stood down in 1922 and the seat was retained for the Conservatives by Thomas Fermor-Hesketh (1881-1944), a prominent Lancashire businessman, educated at Eton and Sandhurst, who had served in the Horse Guards. His tenure was brief, losing in the General Election of 1923 and although he was never again to sit in the Commons, he re-entered Parliament in 1935 as Lord Hesketh. (His grandson, the 3rd Lord Hesketh, attracted attention in the seventies as a sponsor of motor racing and was later to serve as a government minister in the Lords in the Thatcher and Major governments.)

In 1923 the Labour Party took Enfield for the first time and the Liberals fell into insignificance. The successful candidate was William Henderson (1891-1984), son of Arthur Henderson, a key figure in the early Labour Party who held the offices of Home Secretary (1924) and Foreign Secretary (1929-31).

A year later the Conservatives regained Enfield. The new member was Lt. Col. Reginald Applin (1869-1957), who had served in the army 1889-1922 and was the proud author of a book on machine gun tactics. A man of decidedly right wing views, he soon became known as a vehement opponent of women's rights.

In 1929 another General Election brought Labour back to power and in Enfield Henderson snatched

175. Lt. Col. Reginald Applin, Conservative MP for Enfield 1924-9 and 1931-5.

the seat back from Applin. (It is more than likely that women voters, whom Applin professed to despise, played a major part in his downfall.) Henderson held junior ministerial office as Parliamentary Private Secretary to the Secretary of State for India.

In 1931, in the General Election following the formation of the National Government, the Labour Party came close to annihilation. In Enfield, Applin regained the seat for the Conservatives. (Henderson eventually re-entered Parliament in 1945 as Lord Henderson of Westgate and served as junior Foreign Office minister in the Attlee government, his achievements falling sadly short of those of his famous father.) Applin held Enfield until 1935 when, at the age of 66, he decided to stand down. (His last years were spent living in South Africa, where the regime was probably rather more to his taste than that in post-war Britain.)

There was a modest recovery by the Labour Party in the 1935 election but Enfield remained Conservative. The new MP was Bartle Bull (1902-1950), a barrister, who was to hold junior ministerial posts at the Treasury, the Ministry of Transport and the Ministry of Fuel and Power. Then came the landslide victory of Labour in the 1945 election. The new Labour MP, Ernest Davies (1902-1991), was an experienced writer and journalist, who before World War II had had material published by the Left Book Club. From 1946 he held various junior ministerial posts, rising to Under-Secretary of State at the Foreign Office 1950/1951.

In 1950, with the division of the seat into Enfield East and Enfield West, Davies was elected for Enfield East, which he continued to represent until 1959. His parliamentary career ended on a sad note. With his wife seriously ill and not expected to live long, he decided not to contest the seat again and the Enfield East Labour Party selected a new candidate. Then, against the odds, his wife recovered and Davies tried unsuccessfully to find another seat, being narrowly beaten by Tom Driberg for the Labour nomination for Barking. Davies never sat in the Commons again and his death in 1991 went unreported by any of the Enfield local newspapers.

The new MP for Enfield East was John Mackie (1909-1995), a Highland Scot and a farmer by profession. During Harold Wilson's first administration he served as Parliamentary Secretary to the Ministry for Agriculture 1967/1970. After retirement from the Commons in February 1974 he eventually went to the Lords as Lord John-Mackie.

The Enfield West seat newly created in 1950, was won for the Conservatives by Iain Macleod (1913-1970), who at the time of writing remains by far the finest MP ever to have represented an Enfield

176. Iain Macleod, pictured on his election handbill in 1970. Sadly, this was to be his last election campaign and he died barely a month later.

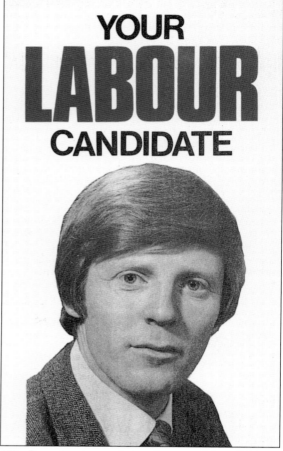

177. Bryan Davies was Labour's successful candidate for Enfield North in 1974.

constituency. Although by birth a Yorkshireman from Skipton, he was by ancestry and temperament a Highland Scot, both parents coming from the Western Isles. In the Commons he soon attracted attention as a fine orator and a formidable debator, one of very few people ever to get the better of Labour's Aneurin Bevan. Physically he was a frail man, suffering much pain from arthritis which seriously affected his neck, spine and shoulders, and, in his latter years, he walked with the aid of a stick. Within two years of entering Parliament he joined the cabinet as Minister of Health, a post he held until 1955 when he became Minister of Labour. His finest achievement was as Colonial Secretary (1959-1961), during which time large parts of Britain's colonial territories gained their independence. Harold Macmillan's wind of change blowing through Africa owed much to the work of Iain Macleod. He subsequently served as Leader of the House of Commons (1961-1963) and then briefly as Conservative Party Chairman. In 1963, when Harold Macmillan resigned as Prime Minister, Macleod refused to serve under his successor, Sir Alec Douglas-Home, not returning to the Conservative front bench until 1965, by which time the party was in opposition. With the Conservative election victory in June 1970 Macleod was appointed Chancellor of the Exchequer in the Heath government, but within a month he was dead. Returning

home after a successful appendicitis operation, he died suddenly from a heart attack just short of his 57th birthday. The highest office of all had eluded him.

In the by-election that followed the Conservatives retained the seat. The new member was Cecil Parkinson (1931-) who was to have a relatively short reign, owing to changes in the constituency boundaries. In the General Election of February 1974 Parkinson opted not to stand for the new Enfield North constituency, but stood (successfully) for Hertfordshire South, which included the Potters Bar area from the old Enfield West seat.

In February 1974 the new Enfield North constituency was won for Labour by Bryan Davies (1939-), a former teacher and lecturer at Middlesex Polytechnic. He served briefly as an assistant government whip before losing his seat in the 1979 General Election. (He eventually returned to the

179. Sir Anthony Berry, MP for Southgate (1964-74) and Enfield-Southgate (1974-84), was killed by an IRA bomb at the Conservative Party Conference at Brighton in 1984.

178. In 1979 Tim Eggar won Enfield North for the Conservatives.

Commons in 1992 as Labour MP for Oldham Central, serving as an opposition spokesman on higher education. Unfortunately, the Oldham Central constituency disappeared as a result of boundary changes and, failing to secure nomination for another seat, Davies left the Commons in 1997.)

Enfield North was won for the Conservatives by Tim Eggar (1951-), who soon established a reputation as a quietly efficient MP, dealing with constituency matters with promptness and unfailing courtesy. He held junior ministerial posts at the Foreign Office, the Department of Education and the Department of Trade and Industry, but the top jobs managed to elude him. Shortly before the General Election of 1997, possibly sensing disaster, he announced his retirement from Parliament. The seat was decisively won back for Labour by Joan Ryan (1955-) who is the first woman ever to represent an Enfield seat in the Commons. (What would Colonel Applin have thought?)

Enfield Southgate, incorporating Cockfosters and Hadley Wood from the old Enfield West seat, elected

(Sir) Anthony Berry (1925-1984) in February 1974. Berry was a member of a distinguished journalistic family, being the son of press baron, Lord Kemsley and the nephew of Lord Camrose, one-time proprietor of *the Daily Telegraph*. He had been Conservative MP for Southgate since 1964. His career was abruptly and tragically terminated in 1984 when he was killed by an IRA bomb at the Conservative Party Conference at Brighton.

In the ensuing by-election the seat was retained for the Conservatives by Michael Portillo (1953-), the son of a Spanish Republican, who had settled in Britain as a refugee after the Spanish Civil War. A protégé of Margaret Thatcher and a staunch supporter of her hard-line right wing policies, he was rapidly rewarded with high office, serving as Chief Secretary to the Treasury, Secretary of State for Employment and Secretary of State for Defence.

In the General Election of 1997 the unthinkable happened. Enfield-Southgate, hitherto regarded as one of the safest Conservative seats in London, was taken by Labour. It is probably too soon to speculate on the reasons for Portillo's defeat, but in retrospect some of his anti-European and other utterances may have been unwise in a constituency containing large numbers of Jewish, Cypriot and Asian voters.

The new MP for Enfield-Southgate was Stephen Twigg (1966-), born in Enfield, an old boy of Southgate School and a former Labour councillor in Islington.

United We Stand ?

To write the history of Enfield in the years since 1965 is a risky business. The events are too recent to be viewed in perspective, too few records are available for research and too many of the participants in the events of the last thirty years are still alive.

The London Borough of Enfield has functioned rather better than might have been expected. The three districts have a great deal of shared history: all three were in the County of Middlesex, the Edmonton Hundred, the Edmonton Poor Law Union and the Enfield Parliamentary Division. On the other hand, one must mention the traditional hostility between Edmonton and Southgate, dating back to the separation of the two districts in 1881. (For a full discussion of that see the author's *Southgate and Edmonton Past*, 1996.) In the present borough there is still an edgy relationship between the mainly working class eastern half and the more affluent districts to the west – this was not so apparent in the days of Enfield's independence.

The new borough was initially controlled by the Labour Party. This first period was marred by controversy over the introduction of comprehensive education (see pp. 91-2). At least partly as a result of this, the 1968 council elections saw a dramatic swing to the Conservatives and the Labour Party reduced to a tiny and ineffectual rump. The Conservatives were to retain control of the authority for 26 years, until Labour came back to power in the 1994 council elections.

The Enfield Civic Centre was completed in 1975, but to a very different design from what had first been contemplated. In order to house the extra staff needed to administer the enlarged borough, a tall stainless steel clad tower block was built alongside the original low-rise building of 1961, tending to dwarf it and to spoil its proportions.

Since 1965 there have been further administrative changes brought about by government legislation. In 1974 the office of Medical Officer of Health was abolished and most of its powers and functions transferred to non-elected health authorities. Thus while environmental health remains a local authority responsibility, health services such as the school medical service and baby clinics were transferred to the health authorities. In 1986 the

Greater London Council was abolished and many of its functions devolved to the boroughs. Locally the GLC-owned Trent Park Estate was transferred to the London Borough of Enfield.

Population, which reached a peak at around 1951, has declined ever since. By 1981 it was reduced by about 9,000 and then stood at 258,770. Since then it has continued to fall but at a slower rate. At the same time it has become ethnically more diverse with the arrival of new immigrant groups who have taken their place alongside older established minorities such as the Jews and the Irish. Significant numbers of Afro-Caribbeans, Asians (both from the Indian sub-continent and East Africa) and black Africans have settled in Enfield.

Recent years have seen large numbers of houses and flats built on virtually any available land including reclaimed land and former industrial sites. Demographic pressures have proved hard to resist. There has been an increasing tendency for young people of childbearing age to settle in Enfield. As a result school rolls and class sizes, both of which had been declining, have suddenly started to climb. At the other end of the spectrum, there is a large increase in the older age groups – consisting mainly of people who moved into Enfield shortly before or shortly after World War II.

Enfield Town had declined as a shopping centre over a long period, but this was reversed in 1982 with the opening of the Palace Gardens Precinct. (A second stage is at the active planning stage.) However, there has recently been established along the Great Cambridge Road what amounts to a completely new shopping centre as the big supermarkets and superstores have taken over former factory sites.

The completion of the M25 in 1984 has markedly improved Enfield's east/west communications. There is a motorway junction with the A10 at Bullsmoor Lane and another just outside the borough boundaries, at Potters Bar.

The long-standing troubles in Northern Ireland spilled over into Enfield. In 1975 wealthy publisher and right wing activist, Ross McWhirter, was gunned down by an IRA gang on the steps of his home in Village Road, Bush Hill Park, shortly after having offered to pay large rewards for information leading to the arrest and conviction of Irish terrorists.

Further Reading

General Works
Victoria County History, Middlesex, Vol. V. (1976).
Hodson, George & Ford, Edward, *A history of Enfield* (1873).
Pam, David, *A history of Enfield*. 3 vols. (1990/94)
Robinson, William, *The history and antiquities of Enfield*, 2 vols. (1823).
Tuff, John, *Historical, topographical and statistical notices of Enfield* (1858).
Whitaker, Cuthbert, *An illustrated historical, statistical and topographical account of Enfield* (1911).

Bush Hill Park
Ford, John Walker, *A sketch towards a history of the neighbourhood: being some particulars of Bush Hill Park* (1904).
Haigh, Douglas, *Old Park in the Manor of Enfield* (1977).
Hoy, Denis, *From fields to flats* (1998).
Robinson, Sidney John, *Sid's family Robinson* (1991).

Enfield Chase
Pam, David, *The story of Enfield Chase* (1984).
Thompson, E.P., *Whigs and hunters: the story of the Black Act* (1975).

Enfield Town
Enfield Preservation Society, *A portrait of Gentleman's Row* (1986).

Forty Hill and Bulls Cross
Edwards, Jack, *The story of Capel* (1985).
Lewis, Norman, *Jackdaw Cake: an autobiography* (1985).
Wilson, Frances, *Memories of Forty Hill* (1947).

Hadley Wood
Clark, Nancy, *Hadley Wood* (1968).

Agrarian History
Middleton, John, *View of the agriculture of Middlesex* (1798).
Burnby, J.G.L. & Robinson, A.E., *Now turned into fair garden plots* (1983).

Archaeology
Gentry, Anne, 'Excavations at Lincoln Road, London Borough of Enfield, November 1974/March 1976', in *LAMAS Trans.* Vol. 28, 1977 pp 101-89.

Gillam, Geoffrey, *Prehistoric and Roman Enfield* (1973).
Ivens, John, *Finds and excavations in Roman Enfield* (1977).

Architecture
Enfield Preservation Society, *Enfield's architectural heritage* (1977).
Royal Commission on Historical Monuments, *An inventory of the historical monuments of Middlesex* (1937).
Gillam, Geoffrey, *Forty Hall, Enfield, 1629-1997* (1997).
Jones, Ian K. & Drayton, Ivy, *The royal palaces of Enfield* (1984).

Co-operative Movement
Smith, H. Charles, *Co-operation in Enfield and its environs* (1932).

Education
Ambrose Fleming School, *Ambrose Fleming School Magazine*: special jubilee issue, 1911-61 (1961).
Collicott, Sylvia, *Enfield School Board* (1985).
Enfield County School Old Girls' Association, Golden jubilee magazine (1959).
Faulkner, Michael J., *St Matthew's C. of E. Primary School 1838-1988* (1988).
Marshall, Leslie Birkett, *A brief history of Enfield Grammar School* (1958).
Sturges, George W., *Schools of the Edmonton Hundred* (1949).
Taylor, R.W, *A history of a school* (1968)

Industry
Enfield Archaeological Society, *Industrial archaeology in Enfield* (1971).
Enfield District Manufacturers' Association, *Industries of Enfield* (1947).

Electrical Manufacturing
Belling & Co. Ltd, *The story of Belling 1911-1962* (1962).
Belling-Lee Ltd, *Golden jubilee, 1922-1972* (1972).
Ediswan Ltd, *The pageant of the lamp* (1949).

Firearms
Ministry of Defence, *British rifles: a catalogue of the Enfield Pattern Room* (1981).
Pam, David, *The Royal Small Arms Factory, Enfield and its workers* (1998).
Reynolds, E.G.B., *The Lee-Enfield Rifle* (1960).

Gas Industry
Merrison, R.W., *A brief account of the Tottenham and District Gas Company's first hundred years, 1847-1947* (1947).

Tottenham & District Gas Co., *Ponders End Works* (1949).

Place Names
Field, John, *Place Names of Greater London* (1980).
English Place-Name Society, *The place-names of Middlesex* (1942).
Dalling, Graham, *A guide to Enfield street names* (1982).

Poor Law
Richardson, Stanley I., *A history of the Edmonton Poor Law Union 1837-1854* (1968).
Graham, Margaret, *The Chase Farm Schools* (1974).

Religion
(Space precludes the listing of histories of individual churches).

General Works:
Mudie-Smith, Richard, *The religious life of London* (1904).

Roman Catholicism
Avery, David, *Popish recusancy in the Elizabethan Hundred of Edmonton* (1968).
Worrall, Edward S., *The Confessor William Le Hunt: priest and schoolmaster* (1962).

Church of England
London and Middlesex Archaeological Society, *Middlesex parish churches* (1955).
Sperling, John Hanson, *Church walks in Middlesex* (1849).

Nonconformity
Knight, Geoffrey, *Nonconformist churches in Enfield* (1973).

Sewerage
Middlesex County Council, *Report on sewerage and sewage disposal in East Middlesex* (1936).
Middlesex County Council, *Inauguration of the East Middlesex main drainage undertaking* (1957).

Theatres and Cinemas
Gillam, Geoffrey, *Theatres, music halls and cinemas in the London Borough of Enfield.*

Trade Unions
Amalgamated Union of Engineers and Foundry Workers, *Some account to 1935 of the Enfield Lock Branch* (1970).

Transport
General works
Barker, T.C. and Robbins, Michael, *A history of London Transport*, 2 vols. (1963/74).
Sekon, G.A., *Locomotion in Victorian London* (1938).

Buses
Blacker, K.C. and others, *London's buses: Vol 1. The independent era, 1922-1934.*

Railways
Allen, Cecil J., *The Great Eastern Railway* (1968).
Croome, Desmond and Jackson, Alan, *Rails through the clay* (1993).
Hill, Jim, *Buckjumbers, gobblers and clauds: a lifetime on Great Eastern and LNER footplates* (1981).
Hodge, Peter, *The Hertford Loop* (1976).
Jackson, Alan, *London's local railways* (1978).
Wrottesley, John, *The Great Northern Railway*, 3 vols. (1979/1981).
Young, John, *Great Northern Suburban* (1977).

Roads
Pam, David, *The Stamford Hill and Green Lanes Turnpike Trust* 2 vols, (1963/4).

Tramways
Smeeton, Cyril S., *The Metropolitan Electric Tramways*, 2 vols. (1984/6).

Waterways
Denney, Martin, *London's Waterways* (1977).
Burnby, J.G.L. and Parker, M., *The navigation of the river Lee 1190-1790* (1978).

War
Enfield Urban District Council, *Enfield victory celebrations, 8 June 1946* (1946).
Gillam, Geoffrey, *Enfield at war 1914-1918* (1982).
Gillam, Geoffrey, *Enfield at war 1939-1945* (1985).
Pluckwell, George, *Children of the war* (1966).

Water Supply
Barry, Septimus, *Some notes concerning the growth and development of water supply and storage in Chingford* (1975).
Dickinson, H.W., *Water supply of Greater London* (1954).
Essex-Lopresti, Michael, *Exploring the New River* (1986).
Gough, J.W., *Sir Hugh Myddelton, entrepreneur and engineer* (1964).
Metropolitan Water Board, *Chingford Reservoir: inauguration by King George V.* (1913).